Keynes' general theory of interest

Foundations of the market economy series
Edited by Mario J. Rizzo, *New York University* and Lawrence H. White, *University of Georgia*

A central theme of this series is the importance of understanding and assessing the market economy from a perspective broader than the static economics of perfect competition and Pareto optimality. Such a perspective sees markets as causal processes generated by the preferences, expectations and beliefs of economic agents. The creative acts of entrepreneurship that uncover new information about preferences, prices and technology are central to these processes. Accordingly, institutional arrangements will be assessed with respect to their ability to promote the discovery and use of knowledge in society. The market economy consists of a set of institutions that facilitate voluntary cooperation and exchange among individuals. These institutions include the legal and ethical framework as well as more narrowly 'economic' patterns of social interaction. Thus the law, legal institutions and cultural or ethical norms, as well as ordinary business practices and monetary phenomena, fall within the analytical domain of the economist.

Keynes' general theory of interest

A reconsideration

Fiona C. Maclachlan

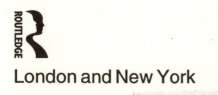

London and New York

First published 1993
by Routledge
11 New Fetter Lane, London EC4P 4EE

Simultaneously published in the USA and Canada
by Routledge
29 West 35th Street, New York, NY 10001

© 1993 Fiona C. Maclachlan

Typeset in Palatino by LaserScript Limited, Mitcham, Surrey
Printed and bound in Great Britain by
Biddles Ltd, Guildford and King's Lynn

British Library Cataloguing in Publication Data
A catalogue reference for this book is available from the British Library

ISBN 0-415-07934-9

Library of Congress Cataloging in Publication Data

Maclachlan, Fiona C. (Fiona Cameron), 1959–
  Keynes' general theory of interest: a reconsideration/Fiona C.
Maclachlan.
  p. cm. – (Foundations of the market economy series)
  Includes bibliographical references and index
  1. Keynes, John Maynard, 1883–1946. – General theory of
employment, interest, and money. 2. Keynesian economics.
3. Interest. 4. Liquidity (Economics) I. Title. II. Series.
HB99.7.K38M33 1993
332.8'2'01–dc20   92-28826
                                                                  CIP
ISBN 0-415-07934-9

Contents

Preface

Today in the sciences, books are usually either texts or retrospective reflections upon one aspect or another of the scientific life. The scientist who writes one is more likely to find his professional reputation impaired than enhanced. Only in the earlier, pre-paradigm, stages of the development of the various sciences did the book ordinarily possess the same relation to professional achievement that it still retains in other creative fields. And only in those fields that still retain the book, with or without the article, as a vehicle for research communication are the lines of professionalization still so loosely drawn that the layman may hope to follow progress by reading the practitioners' original reports.

(Thomas Kuhn 1970: 20)

Today in economics, as in the hard sciences, the mathematical model written up succinctly in the form of a journal article is the preferred means of scientific communication. To write an entire book in basic economic theory betrays in the author either an ignorance of the accepted conventions, or a conviction that these conventions are inappropriate for the topic under investigation. It is my belief that the theory of interest is in a highly unsettled state requiring a reexamination of the fundamental issues. Until the fundamental issues are resolved, the mathematical models and empirical studies are liable to miss the mark. The present work aims to be constructive rather than critical: a systematic critique of the 'mainstream' view is not attempted. Rather, a competing view is developed and defended. It is hoped that even if I fail to persuade readers of my view, they will be stimulated to consider more deeply the challenges involved in interest rate theory.

The present work is a revised version of my PhD dissertation submitted at New York University. Its beginning can be traced to my noticing an intriguing parallel between elements of Keynes' liquidity preference theory of interest and the Austrian pure time preference theory. The fact that the same idea arose from two independent sources suggested it might be worth pursuing. The result was a reconsideration of Keynes' insights on the interest rate and an attempt to provide them with a stronger theoretical justification than Keynes himself had given them. However, the book should not be construed as an exegesis of Keynes. My primary concern is not Keynes' true meaning and much of what follows is bound to irritate the fundamentalist Keynesian scholar. Nor should the book be construed as an encyclopaedic account of the literature on liquidity preference. Failure on my part to mention any particular contribution means only that I did not judge it directly relevant to the thesis I am defending and should not be considered a reflection of its importance.

The book represents the product of many years of graduate study and a debt is owed to several excellent teachers. Paul Davidson's ground-breaking work led me to see some of the limitations of mainstream thinking in monetary theory. His influence on the role of uncertain expectations and historical time in economic analysis should be obvious in the following pages. Also at Rutgers, the late Alfred S. Eichner taught me the importance of allowing real world economic institutions, rather than current theoretical fashions, to guide one's theory construction. Eichner's commitment to disinterested research, his unselfish efforts on behalf of students, and his enviable affability in the face of superficial criticism made him a teacher of rare personal quality. His untimely death was a great loss.

At New York University I found a congenial environment for independent research in the Austrian programme. A fellowship freed time for the extensive reading and thinking that a project of this sort requires. The weekly Austrian colloquium provided me with a valuable testing ground for each of the chapters that follows. The serious consideration and lively debate that met my ideas there stimulated many improvements. Israel M. Kirzner, who served as my principal dissertation advisor, applied a high standard of rigour which I worked hard to achieve. His willingness to see the project through, despite its conflict with his own views on the subject, was in the true spirit of scholarship.

Mario Rizzo's sympathetic and open-minded reading of the dissertation led him to see many ways in which it could be strengthened. I also benefitted enormously from Lawrence H. White's careful scrutiny of an early attempt at the topic. His insightful comments led to important modifications in the formative stages. Also contributing useful comments in the various stages of the production of this work were Peter Boettke, Robin Cowan, Paul Davidson, Alan Jarvis, the late Ludwig Lachmann, Gary Mongiovi, Ingo Pellengahr, Jonas Prager and two anonymous referees. As I did not always heed the advice I was given, I assume full responsibility for all remaining errors.

Finally, I would like to thank my husband Marcos for his unwavering support during what must have seemed an endless venture. Our children, Margaret and Simon, were not always as supportive, but they can be thanked, at least, for forcing my energies into a healthy balance during the writing of this book.

Chapter 1

Introduction

The theory of interest has for a long time been a weak spot in the science of economics, and the explanation and determination of the interest rate still gives rise to more disagreement among economists than any other branch of general economic theory.

(Gottfried Haberler [1939] 1958: 195)

Following the marginalist revolution of the late nineteenth century, economists were able to reach an unprecedented degree of consensus about the basic principles of the determination of price in a competitive market economy. Yet when these general principles were applied in the explanation of the rate of interest, the result was a set of several distinct theories. Controversy continued to rage over the rudimentary question of the ultimate cause of interest: was it due solely to time preference (Fetter [1914] 1977), or to the productivity of capital (Brown 1913, 1914), or to both (Fisher 1907, 1930)? Eventually, the debate subsided and Fisher's theory came to dominate in textbook presentations; but many of the issues were never adequately resolved. As a result, controversy brewed again when the Cambridge, England critics of neoclassical capital and interest theory pointed to logical defects in the standard textbook treatment.

Within the controversy, the liquidity preference theory of interest has played a very limited role. In Daniel Hausman's (1981) thorough study of modern interest rate theory, for instance, it is not mentioned at all. 'It seems that the liquidity preference theory of the rate of interest is now widely regarded as either unimportant, incorrect or both' (McGregor 1985: 89). The theory survives to a certain extent in macroeconomic theory, but it has been neglected by economists studying the fundamental problems of value and distribution.

In the following work, we hope to show that the liquidity preference theory that was imperfectly set out by Keynes in his *General Theory* and subsequent articles, deserves a place in any serious debate about the theory of interest. Our primary aim is not to determine what Keynes really said, but rather to attempt a rational reconstruction of his theory. Keynes' work provides the inspiration but the end result bears a debatable resemblance to his seminal contribution. The issue of whether our restatement of the liquidity preference theory is consistent with Keynes' original intention is one that we consider subsidiary to our central thesis and will be dealt with separately in a later chapter.

AN OVERVIEW OF THE LITERATURE ON LIQUIDITY PREFERENCE

For many economists, the strongest association with the liquidity preference theory is the IS–LM model. The model has proven much more resilient than Keynes' original writings and the theory of interest implicit in the model has eclipsed Keynes' suggestive prose presentation of his own theory. The exact origins of the model are not clear (Young 1987) but Hicks is justly credited with popularizing it in his 1937 article, 'Mr Keynes and the Classics', in which Hicks complains that in his original exposition of the theory, Keynes did not adequately capture the interdependence that exists between his key variables. Keynes organizes the theory into a series of sequential steps and summarizes his theory as saying:

1 the money supply in relation to the state of liquidity preference determines the interest rate;
2 the rate of interest in relation to the marginal efficiency of capital determines the level of investment; and
3 the level of investment together with the marginal propensity to consume determines the level of aggregate income.

Hicks notes, however, that since Keynes is using the term liquidity preference to refer to the total demand for money and since the total demand for money depends on the level of income, the theory is circular. Hicks sets about to remedy the circularity in the reasoning by casting the argument in the form of simultaneous equations. His IS–LM model can be represented as a system of two equations in two unknowns:

$$M^{3s} = L(r, Y)$$
$$I(r, Y) = S(r, Y)$$

where M^{3s} is the supply of money, $L()$ is the demand for money, r the rate of interest, Y the level of income, I the level of investment, and S the level of saving. The second equation is supposed to represent equilibrium in the goods market. Unlike conventional general equilibrium models in which individual prices adjust to clear the goods markets, Hicks' IS–LM model has the peculiar feature that all prices except the interest rate are taken as given. Thus, it is only through adjustments in income and the interest rate that equilibrium in the goods markets is restored. The model suggests that if the market for pizza ovens, say, is out of equilibrium then equilibrium will be restored through an adjustment in the interest rate and incomes which in turn react on the amount of saving. It is not clear, however, that a mechanism equilibrating saving and investment is part of Keynes' original system. In Keynes' theory '(*ex ante*) saving and investment *are not brought into equality by anything whatever*, save the purest accident. For they do not confront each other simultaneously in one and the same market' (Shackle 1967: 239). A disaggregated view has equilibrium in the pizza oven market achieved essentially through an adjustment in the prices or quantities, or both, of pizza ovens. Any effect on saving is likely to be indirect and weak: it will not be central in the equilibrating process.

Yet despite this seemingly obvious criticism of the model, Keynes did not object to Hicks' 1937 paper. He wrote to Hicks about a draft of the article: 'At long last I have caught up with my reading and have been through the enclosed. I found it very interesting and really have next to nothing to say by way of criticism' (Keynes [1937] 1973, 14: 79). The reaction is ambiguous. The term 'interesting' can be used as a compliment or it can be used as a way of evading saying something more definite, either negative or positive. It is certainly not a ringing endorsement. Keynes' not wanting to present criticisms might indicate that he accepted it but it might also mean that he did not want to be bothered to devote the careful thought necessary to discover any defect. At the time Keynes was under the gun of a great many critics. He may have chosen to let Hicks' paper pass without serious scrutiny because Hicks could be counted as a supporter: with so many dissenters to deal with, it might not have seemed worthwhile to find fault with a follower.

In any event, there appear to be several aspects of the IS–LM model that are inconsistent with Keynes' original position. Besides the use of the condition that savings equal investment to represent equilibrium in the goods market that we have already mentioned, there is Hicks' use of the liquidity trap to explain Keynes' insistence that the interest rate determines the marginal efficiency of capital and not *vice versa*. Hicks claims that Keynes' result is properly regarded as a special case of his theory that obtains only when the LM curve is horizontal, that is, only in the case in which the demand for money is infinitely elastic. Keynes (1936: 207), however, had discussed the liquidity trap and concluded that although it was a possibility, it had never occurred. It seems implausible, then, that it was the liquidity trap that he had in mind when he denied that the marginal efficiency of capital determines the interest rate.

Another aspect of the IS–LM model that appears inconsistent with Keynes is its neglect of the causal process through which the interest rate is determined. In a simultaneous equation model the question of the 'determination' of a variable is simply the mathematical question of which value of the variable simultaneously satisfies all the equations. It leaves to the side all questions of what actually happens in which markets to cause the variable to take on a particular value. Pasinetti (1974: 46) says that Hicks 'has in fact broken up Keynes' basic chain of arguments. The relations have been turned into a system of simultaneous equations, i.e., precisely what Keynes did not want them to be'. In order to properly represent a causal process, one needs to abandon the simultaneous equation approach and frame one's theory in the context of historical time.

Hicks was later to express reservations about his 1937 article. Interestingly, the problem he points to is the way in which the model abstracts from time.

> I must say that [IS–LM] is now much less popular with me than I think it still is with many other people. It reduces the *General Theory* to equilibrium economics; it is not really *in* time. That, of course, is why it has done so well.
>
> (Hicks [1976] 1983: 289–90)

Hicks explains that there are two sides to Keynes' theory. One side dealing with liquidity preference and the marginal efficiency of capital which is 'unquestionably *in time*' (*op. cit.*: 289), and the multiplier theory which, like equilibrium economics, is out of time. Hicks argues that it was the latter side that had been developed by Keynes' successors while the former side was neglected.

> The 'Keynesian revolution' went off at half-cock; so the line, which I believe to be a vital line, was smudged over. The equilibrists . . . thought that what Keynes had said could be absorbed into their equilibrium systems; all that was needed was that the scope of their equilibrium systems should be extended. As we know, there has been a lot of extension, a vast amount of extension; what I am saying is that it has never quite got to the point.
>
> (*op. cit.*: 289)

The vast amount of extension to the IS–LM model to which Hicks refers begins with Modigliani's seminal 1944 article. In the article, Modigliani (1944: 48) states his main task to be 'to clarify and develop [Hicks'] arguments taking into account later theoretical developments.' The major improvement made by Modigliani was his relaxation of Hicks' assumption of rigid real wages. In doing so, he reached the startling conclusion that if real wages are flexible, then liquidity preference does not determine the interest rate. Rather the interest rate is determined purely by real, or non-monetary, factors.

Modigliani's version of the IS–LM model consists of the following equations:

1   $X = F(N)$
2   $W/P = F'(N)$
3   $N = N(W/P)$
4   $S = S(r, W/P, X)$
5   $I = I(r, W/P, X)$
6   $S = I$
7   $M^s = L(r, WP/W, X)$

Where X is aggregate output, N is aggregate employment, $F()$ is the production function with a given stock of capital, $N()$ is the labour supply function, W is the nominal wage rate, P is the price level, S is saving, I is investment, M^s is the money supply and $L()$

is the demand for money. The model is structured so that it can be divided into three separate sub-systems (Hahn 1955: 55) with 1–3 determining X, N, and W/P; 4–6 determining S, I, and r; and 7 determining P.

It is on the basis of this feature of the model that Modigliani reaches the conclusion that saving and investment determine the interest rate and liquidity preference determines the price level. There is some ambiguity, however, with the term 'determines', as we have mentioned already. The theory that Keynes was attacking in the *General Theory* was one that suggested that saving and investment play a *causal* role in the determination of the interest rate. Within Modigliani's model, on the other hand, determination has a mathematical meaning that does not necessarily imply any causality. It is only in Modigliani's verbal discussion that he reveals his belief that the interest rate is determined in the causal, as well as the mathematical, sense by saving and investment, independently of monetary factors. He buttresses the result of his model with three verbal arguments.

The first arises in his discussion of long-run equilibrium. He defines it to be a state in which the quantity of money that people desire to hold as a store of wealth is constant (Modigliani 1944: 60). The implication is that in long-run equilibrium, wealth-holders cease to be operative figures in the loanable funds market and hence have no effect on the interest rate. Modigliani successfully rules out any long-run monetary effect on the interest rate through his choice of a definition of long-run equilibrium. But the question of the appropriateness of his definition arises. It might be plausible to define a long-run equilibrium as a state in which markets clear because there are tendencies pushing the economy in that direction. But there are no similar tendencies causing wealth-holders to hold onto a fixed amount of money as a store of wealth. As long as there is uncertainty about future rates of interest, there will be the possibility of variable levels of speculative balances, and there are no apparent tendencies towards certain expectations of the course of future rates. The environment in which wealth-holders make their decisions is inherently uncertain and in a constant state of flux. In eliminating that flux, Modigliani's definition of long-run equilibrium may be abstracting from an important feature of the loanable funds market.

The second verbal argument presented by Modigliani takes

the form of a conceptual experiment of the type we shall employ in Chapter 4. He supposes that the marginal efficiency of capital falls from r_0 to r_1 and asks about the process through which equilibrium is restored. He then asserts – without explanation – that in 'order for the system to reach a new position of equilibrium, it is necessary that the interest rate fall to $[r_1]$' (1944: 72). In saying so he is admitting that he believes the marginal efficiency of capital directly determines the interest rate. He ignores the possibility that the causality might run the other way and that the equilibrating process would involve either a reduction in the level of investment or a fall in the price of investment goods, both of which would cause the marginal efficiency of capital to rise back up towards r_0.

The third argument used by Modigliani to support his conclusion that the interest rate is determined by saving and investment involves the presentation of some empirical evidence. He notes that in developed countries with high rates of saving and capital accumulation, interest rates are low; while in the less developed countries in which savings rates and the level of capital accumulation are lower, interest rates are high. This empirical evidence is far from conclusive, however, since other factors can be adduced to explain the discrepancy. One can cite at least three:

1 in less developed countries there is a greater degree of distrust in the central monetary authority's commitment to keeping inflation under control and thus a higher inflationary premium is built into the interest rate;
2 in less developed countries there are fewer established and credit-worthy firms and thus the risk-premia are bound to be higher on average; and
3 lenders in less developed countries do not have the same access to reliable sources of information about credit-worthiness and will add a margin onto the interest rate to compensate for the uncertainty.

Modigliani's 1944 version of the IS–LM model stimulated criticism which led to improvements. The criticism, however, is not along the lines of our observations above. Rather than being concerned with his substantive conclusion about the role of monetary factors in the determination of the interest rate, the criticism is about the logical structure of the model. Patinkin

(1948, 1949) questions Modigliani's assertion that the price level is determined by the money equation alone, while all the other variables are determined independently of the money equation. Patinkin argues that if money is allowed in the utility function so that it is a substitute for the other goods entering the utility function, then the demand for at least one good must depend on the absolute price level. If a change in the price level does not affect the demand for any other good, as Modigliani supposes, then it must mean that the amount of money people hold is always the equilibrium amount regardless of the price level. If that is the case, however, then the money equation cannot be used to determine the price level.

Hahn (1955) presents a similar argument. He notes that Walras's Law implies that the value of total demand for goods and money must be equal to the value of their total supply and concludes that it 'is therefore of considerable importance to [Modigliani's] model to make certain that it is not also true that the total demand for everything excluding money is identically equal to the total supply of everything excluding money', that is, that Say's Law does not hold. For if Say's Law holds then 'we would have no equation (as distinct from an identity) to determine the absolute level of prices' (Hahn 1955: 56). However, if Say's Law does not hold and if, as Modigliani supposes, there is a price level that will clear the money market without any effect on the real sector, then at that price level, Walras's Law does not hold.

Modigliani (1963) answers these objections by presenting a more sophisticated version of his 1944 IS–LM model. He says that the two models are 'basically identical in spirit' (1963: 79) but lists several improvements in the later model, including a more explicit general equilibrium formulation of the theory and a recasting of the mathematical functions representing consumption, investment and the demand for money. Within the extended IS–LM model, the interest rate is no longer determined by the savings and investment equation alone but, like other prices in a general equilibrium model, is determined simultaneously by all the excess demand equations. In fact, one could argue that within the context of the improved IS–LM model there is no liquidity preference theory of interest. If it has any meaning at all it can only be as a theoretically inferior partial equilibrium theory.

Modigliani's later model gained wide acceptance among

macroeconomists. Advances were made but they were made within the basic framework of the IS–LM model. One of the major areas of research on liquidity preference centred on the specification of the money demand function and on its micro-foundations. Tobin's (1958) model of the speculative motive for holding money is probably the most famous extension of Keynes' liquidity preference theory. Tobin begins by attributing to Keynes the assumption that investors hold their predictions of the future rate of interest with certainty. Tobin writes that 'when [Keynes] refers to uncertainty in the market, he appears to mean disagreement amongst investors concerning the future of the rate rather than subjective doubt in the mind of an individual investor' (Tobin 1958: 70). The interpretation seems inconsistent, however, with Keynes' ([1937] 1973, 14: 113) stated view that 'our knowledge of the future is fluctuating, vague and uncertain'. It would be more accurate to say that Keynes allowed for both types of uncertainty.

The implication of Tobin's interpretation is that an investor in Keynes' theory will hold a portfolio of only bonds or only money. If he believes with certainty that the future interest rate will be above the current rate, he will hold only money, and if he believes with certainty that it will be below, he will hold only bonds. Tobin seeks to replace what he takes to be Keynes' account of the speculative motive with one that predicts more realistically a diversification in the portfolios of individual investors. He assumes that an investor bases his portfolio decision on a subjectively determined probability distribution of the capital gain from holding a bond. A positive capital gain is associated with a reduction in the rate of interest and a negative capital gain is associated with an increase in the rate of interest. Thus, while the investor would not claim to know the future rate of interest, he would claim to know the probability of it falling within a given range. The variance of the subjectively determined distribution is construed as the risk associated with holding a bond.

Tobin shows that if the investor's utility function is such that increasing risk yields decreasing utility at an increasing rate and that increasing return yields increasing utility at a decreasing rate, then he will maximize his utility by diversifying between money and bonds. In the general model, Tobin does not give the utility function a specific form so it is impossible to derive an explicit demand function for speculative balances. His model stimulated the search for an expected utility function that exhibits a positive Arrow–Pratt measure of risk aversion and shows that for a given rate of return the investor prefers a lower variance in his portfolio to a higher one. Two utility functions were found that satisfy both criteria – the constant absolute risk aversion function and the quadratic utility function – but both carry with them unrealistic implications about investor behaviour (Cuthbertson 1985: 45–6).

While the Modigliani–Tobin interpretation of Keynes' liquidity preference theory is arguably the dominant one, dissenters from that tradition can be found. The dissenters are not an homogeneous group but many share the belief that a general equilibrium model is an inappropriate framework for Keynes' theories. A full account of the liquidity preference theory, they maintain, requires more than the specification of a set of equations whose simultaneous solution yields a value for the interest rate. Rather, they prefer an explanation framed in historical time. Moreover, they reject the assumption that one can represent behaviour in the face of uncertainty as behaviour in the face of known probability distributions, or even known means and variances.

Despite areas of agreement, however, the dissenters can be divided into two opposing camps. On the one side are those who believe that the liquidity preference theory, properly interpreted, constitutes a complete explanation of interest. Opposing them is a second camp which maintains that the liquidity preference theory, by itself, is incomplete and needs to be buttressed by a theory linking the interest rate to non-monetary factors. The first group rejects the widely held position that liquidity preference is only a short-run explanation. Most notable in this small group are Shackle (1949, 1967, 1972, 1974), Kahn (1954) and Townshend (1937). Rather than viewing liquidity preference as transitory, these economists tend to view it as an ever-present response to a pervasive uncertainty and they regard as irrelevant any theory that abstracts from it. Shackle (1949: 116), for instance, writes that the 'rate of interest is, of all prices, the one most inseparably bound up by the logic of its very nature with expectation and uncertainty. These are, indeed, the main reason for its existence'.

This first group tends to put more emphasis on the theory of interest as it is presented in Chapter 17 of the *General Theory* and in Keynes' post-*General Theory* articles than in other parts of his work. In particular, they reject the suggestion in the *General Theory* (Keynes 1936: 171) that has been incorporated into the IS–LM interpretation, of a stable money demand function. Shackle writes:

> The essence of the liquidity theory, its ascription of interest to uncertainty and the speculative motive, are considerably obscured by the *General Theory*'s retrograde resort to the notion of a stable curve relating the size of the money stock to the interest rate. The appeal to a supposedly stable curve is, perhaps, merely didactic, but liable to be highly misleading.
>
> (Shackle 1972: vi)

Similarly, Kahn writes:

> Sufficient has been said to demonstrate the unsuitability of thinking of a schedule of liquidity preference as though it could be represented by a well-defined curve or by a functional relationship expressed in mathematical terms or subject to econometric processes. Keynes himself often gave way to the temptation to picture the state of liquidity preference as a fairly stable relationship, despite his intuitional horror of undue formalism, but his treatment at least can be justified by the need at the time for a forceful and clear-cut exposition if it was to carry any weight at all.
>
> (Kahn 1954: 250)

For Kahn and Shackle, expectations are highly volatile and reactive to changes in the interest rate. Thus any movement along a demand for money curve would be bound to bring with it a change in the state of expectation and hence a change in the position of the curve. As a consequence they believe it inadmissible to adopt the *ceteris paribus* condition which underlies a money demand curve that expectations are constant.

Another point on which the first group stands apart from the mainstream interpretation of the liquidity preference theory is in their endorsement of Keynes' Chapter 17 argument that the money rate of interest determines the level of the marginal efficiency of capital. Here they break from the microtheorists who abstract from money in order to determine the real or natural rate of interest and who assert that in equilibrium the real rate determines the money rate. They also break from the macrotheorists who present a general equilibrium system in which the marginal efficiency of capital and the money rate are determined jointly.

Like Keynes, however, the first group is not very successful in providing a convincing argument that the causality runs from monetary to real factors. Economists are accustomed to regarding economic variables as interdependent and statements about unidirectional causality raise suspicion (Johnson 1961: 4). There is no doubt that the real factors of capital productivity and time preference come into play in the loanable funds market, so one is naturally led to wonder how they can be ignored. Shackle (1974: 56) writes that Keynes 'is describing a speculative market, whose whole nature and mode of life consists in the holding of opposite views by two camps about what the impending price-movement will be, and in the attainment of momentary stillness by means of an actual price-movement which transfers some members from one camp to the other.' Yet he gives little indication as to why the actions of savers and investors are unimportant. Similarly, Kahn (1954: 238) writes that the 'quantity of money is the means by which the public holds that part of their wealth which is looked after by the banking system. The prices of securities are such as to secure a home for all of them with the public, apart from what the banking system looks after itself.' Here Kahn suggests that wealth-holders are the important ones in determining the prices of securities, but again with no justification.

The second group of dissenters from the IS–LM tradition in the liquidity preference literature rejects liquidity preference as a complete explanation of the rate of interest. There is some variation, however, in what is thought to be missing in the liquidity preference theory. On the one hand, there are those who agree with Leijonhufvud (1968: 213) that liquidity preference can explain only short-run movements of the interest rate about some average level but that it cannot explain the average level, or with Robinson (1961: 598) that liquidity preference does not provide sufficient reason for the existence of interest. But then there are those who take the position advanced by Kaldor (1960) that liquidity preference can explain only the short-term rate of interest, and that another explanation is necessary for the long-term rate. The short-term rate is construed as being determined by speculation about the long-term rate, while the long-term rate is determined by separate factors. Still another view (held as well by some proponents of IS–LM) is that liquidity preference can explain the differential between the short-term and the long-term rate of interest but that it cannot explain the short-term rate (Mott 1985–6: 230).

Neither of the two groups of dissenters from IS–LM represent much of an advance on what is in Keynes. The second group tries, in fact, to limit him by denying his claim that he has presented a complete theory of interest. The first group has succeeded in making a few issues clearer but has had very little impact on the profession. The reason is most likely the unavoidable vagueness that attends their theory. It does not lend itself to precise mathematical formalisms or econometric tests.[1] Moreover, their work tends to be interpretive rather than original, and thus is relegated to the domain of history of economic thought.

Our brief overview of the literature on liquidity preference has divided the workers in the field into three roughly drawn groups. The first and largest are those working within the context of the IS–LM. Their work centres primarily on extending and formalizing the function for the demand for money. A second much smaller and less influential group defends Keynes' original exposition of his liquidity preference theory. If the present work had to be classified it would fit best, although imperfectly, within this group. The third group that we identify rejects both the IS–LM interpretation and Keynes' claim to have offered, in his liquidity preference theory, a complete explanation of the rate of interest. This third group does allow, however, that liquidity preference plays at least some role in the explanation.

The three groups embrace most of the economists with some sympathy for the liquidity preference theory. Economists who are unsympathetic probably form a larger segment of the population and separate out into many more groups. Since our aim is to present a new statement of the theory, an analysis of the reasons economists have given for rejecting old statements seems unnecessary. One criticism that may be worth discussing, however, is the one put forward by many Post Keynesians. Post Keynesians are generally sympathetic to Keynes' work but many (e.g. Lavoie 1984; Moore 1988) reject the liquidity preference theory on the grounds that it involves the assumption of an exogenous money supply. They argue that in a modern credit economy, the money supply is created by the demand so that any change in demand automatically brings about a change in the supply. The idea of the interest rate as the price coordinating the demand and supply of money is, thus, rejected. The usual procedure of regarding the money supply as exogenous and the interest rate as endogenous is reversed so that the interest rate becomes the exogenous variable.

In the Post Keynesian literature, there are two separate reasons for treating the interest rate as exogenous. One is that the interest rate can be regarded as a policy variable that is set by the central bank (Moore 1988). The other reason is that since '[the interest rate] is expectational, subjective, psychic and indeterminate' (Shackle quoted in Rogers 1989: 16), it is beyond the bounds of economic theory. We reject as unrealistic the first reason that the interest rate is fully determined by central bank policy.[2] The second reason is less controversial, in our view. We agree that conventional neoclassical tools may be inadequate for developing a theory of interest, but we do not agree with the implication that the interest rate must be taken as an exogenous variable. Our position is that a theory of interest, of some sort, should be produced. In the end, one might conclude with Pasinetti (1974: 47), that the rate of interest is 'determined *exogenously* with respect to the income generation process'. But if one wants to persuade someone who takes a different view to accept this conclusion, it is necessary to be able to produce a theory to support it.

Not all Post Keynesians are willing to discard the liquidity preference theory on the grounds that the money supply is endogenously determined. Wray (1990), for instance, argues that the liquidity preference theory of interest is compatible with endogenous money. He draws the distinction between the demand for money, which he defines as the willingness to issue debt to finance spending and liquidity preference, which he defines as the desire to exchange illiquid items in a balance sheet with more liquid items. His argument is that money demand which relates to the flow of spending in the economy does not directly affect interest rates since banks can accommodate to it. Liquidity preference, on the other hand, relating to the desired level of stocks on the part of 'surplus units' and banks, does affect interest rates. Wray's synthesis of endogenous money and liquidity preference bears some relation to the one that will be presented here. Like Wray, we shall argue that the motivations of the surplus units, or wealth-holders as we call them, play a critical role in the determination of the interest rate. The important difference between the analyses, however, is in the reason we give for down playing the role of changes in spending flows. While we allow for some responsiveness in the supply of money, we reject the assumption that the supply of bank money is perfectly elastic. Instead, we present an alternative argument to show why changes in the demand for money on the part of consumers and producers will exert little direct influence on the rate of interest (Chapter 4).

THE LIQUIDITY PREFERENCE THEORY RESTATED: A PREVIEW

The methodology that we employ breaks from the standard IS–LM tradition in Keynesian scholarship. Rather than relying on a simultaneous equation model, the solution to which provides insight into the mathematical relationship between variables in a state of equilibrium, we adopt a causal mode of explanation. An attempt is made to construct a causal chain tracing the phenomenon of interest back to its roots in individual preferences. The emphasis is placed not so much on characterizing a state of general equilibrium, as on elucidating the processes through which equilibria in individual markets are approached.

The starting point for any liquidity preference theory is to define interest in the everyday sense as the percentage premium with which a present unit of account denominated claim – that is, money – exchanges with a future unit of account denominated claim. Immediately, in defining interest in this way, the liquidity preference theorist breaks from a long tradition in interest rate theory of abstracting from money and choosing to explain a postulated natural or real rate of interest. For a long time, economists have followed J.S. Mill's ([1848] 1909: 488) teaching that there 'cannot . . . be intrinsically a more insignificant thing, in the economy of society, than money'. The result has been a prejudice among theorists against monetary theories of interest. Knight (1941: 64) was typical in dismissing Keynes' liquidity preference theory as 'mere man-on-the-street economics'.

While it is true that a crudely formulated monetary theory of interest can contain a nominalist fallacy, we maintain the possibility of a valid theory that makes explicit recognition of the fact that loan contracts are denominated in the unit of account.

The reluctance of value theorists to develop a monetary theory of interest and their rush to abstract from money has led them, we believe, to overlook the motive of liquidity preference. It is not a motive that has been considered and then dismissed as insignificant; rather, because of the way in which theories of value and distribution have been structured, it is a motive that has been entirely ignored.

Among macroeconomists, liquidity preference is usually viewed as a demand for money or real balances. Our restatement departs from the standard treatment and interprets liquidity preference as an incentive that may lie behind a demand for money. We begin by defining liquidity as a subjectively determined attribute that reflects both the degree of certainty that one has about an asset's future purchasing power and one's expectation of the transactions costs involved in transforming it into immediate purchasing power. The motive of liquidity preference – that is, the preference for more over less liquidity in one's assets – we argue, is the result of the common desire in an uncertain world to keep one's options open. Interest, then, is the amount that must be paid to compensate one for the loss of liquidity associated with trading a present claim for a future one.

In the first part of our restatement, we approach the question of the determination of the rate of interest in a general way. We look for what we call, following Böhm-Bawerk ([1914] 1959), the originating cause of interest. We define an originating cause to be something that meets two conditions: its existence is always associated with the existence of interest and it cannot itself be the result of interest. We find that unlike the productivity of capital and the preference for present over future consumption, liquidity preference meets both conditions. Although the discussion of the originating cause of interest does not constitute a complete theory, it serves as a useful preliminary. It clears the ground and points the way for a theory in which liquidity preference plays a part. But its main purpose is to refute the commonly-held notion that liquidity preference can only be a short-run explanation, in the sense that liquidity preference may cause fluctuations in the rate of interest but that it cannot explain why it exists.

In the second part of our restatement, we attempt to work out the links in the causal chain that connect the motive of liquidity preference to the rate of interest that is observed. We first explore the notion of speculative trading and present an empirical postulate about the behaviour of wealth-holders. The postulate says that given a change in the real conditions in the loanable funds market, any direct effect on the interest rate can be swamped in the short-run by the reaction of speculative wealth-holders. We argue that the postulate is plausible in an economy in which the quantity of outstanding debt that is traded is large relative to the flow of new issues and new savings.

To elucidate the causal process through which the interest rate might be determined we introduce changes in the various factors operating in the loanable funds market and then investigate how the market process might work itself out. We examine changes in the productivity of capital, in the preference for present over future consumption and in liquidity preference. We find that given the assumptions of our model, changes in the real factors of productivity and thrift need not have any direct effect on the rate of interest. The absence of an effect in the short-run follows from our empirical postulate about wealth-holder behaviour. In the long-run, the result follows from the possibility that equilibrium in the affected real sectors can be restored through price and quantity adjustments of the relevant markets. The restoration of equilibrium need not require any adjustment of the interest rate. A disequilibrium resulting from changes in liquidity preference, on the other hand, can only be restored through a change in the interest rate. Our conclusion is that the interest rate appearing in the market is more likely to be the result of the motives of wealth-holders, than of the motives of producers or consumers.

Once our restatement of the liquidity preference theory is set out in full, we turn to Keynes and examine closely his writings on the theory of interest. We argue that although his exposition of the liquidity preference theory is flawed and full of inconsistencies, there is evidence that he had an intuitive grasp of the basic insights of a valid theory. In Chapter 6, we discuss the liquidity preference versus loanable funds debate. The debate provides a good vehicle for examining how the liquidity preference theory of interest has been received by the economics profession. Many of Keynes' contemporaries were critical on the grounds that Keynes did not appear to be saying anything new. The liquidity preference theory appeared to them not to offer anything different in substance from what could be found in the loanable funds theory. Before this first stage in the debate had been resolved, however, the focus shifted as the two theories were given a mathematical general equilibrium interpretation. In the second stage of the debate, Keynes' original insights seemed to have got lost. As a result, the liquidity preference was unjustly discredited in the minds of most economists.

We complete the book by drawing out some of the macroeconomic implications of a liquidity preference theory. The traditional view of the interest rate coordinating saving and investment, which for a while was out of fashion, now dominates in discussion of policy issues. We analyse in detail the concept of intertemporal coordination that lies behind much of the current thinking. An acceptance of a liquidity preference theory of interest is shown to require a different approach to the issues associated with saving and accumulation.

Chapter 2

Methodology and definitions

METHODOLOGY

Frank Hahn (Addleson 1986: 4) reduces neoclassical economics to three elements. They are reductionism or the 'attempt to locate explanations in the actions of individual agents', an acceptance of 'some axioms of rationality' as a basis for theorizing about agents, and the view that 'some notion of equilibrium is required and that the study of the equilibrium state is useful'. Under this broad definition and given a loose interpretation of the 'equilibrium state', the methodology that we shall employ in our restatement of the liquidity preference theory of interest could be classified as neoclassical. And yet, in many respects it departs from the main-stream neoclassical theorizing that one finds in leading journals.

Much of the work done today in neoclassical economics adopts what we might call a 'general equilibrium' approach. The approach has its roots in the work of Walras who was one of the first to introduce the idea of modelling the economy by means of simultaneous equations, creating what Schumpeter (1954: 827) has described as 'the only work by an economist that will stand comparison with the achievements of theoretical physics . . . the outstanding landmark on the road that economics travels toward the status of a rigorous or exact science'. The general equilibrium approach can be found today in the disaggregated models employed by microeconomists (see Arrow and Hahn 1971), as well as in the aggregated versions employed by macroeconomists (see Sargent 1979).

Typically, a general equilibrium theory proceeds by:

1 postulating a set of optimization problems that agents in the economy are supposedly solving;

2 deriving the equilibrium conditions stating the relationships
   between economic variables that must hold if the agents have
   successfully optimized and markets have cleared; and
3 solving the system of simultaneous equilibrium conditions to
   determine the values of the economic variables in terms of the
   parameters of the agents' optimization problems.

The 'results' of the theory are usually mathematical expressions
of the equilibrium relationships between the economic, or endogenous, variables and the exogenous parameters of the
system. These mathematical relationships are sometimes construed as falsifiable predictions (Friedman 1953; Hahn 1973).

In discussions of types of neoclassical economics, a distinction
is sometimes made between Walras's approach and Marshall's
partial equilibrium analysis. Methodologically, however, the
approach is essentially the same. A partial equilibrium theory, as
it is interpreted in mainstream economics, is nothing more than
a general equilibrium theory with some of the economic
variables set as constants (Stiglitz 1977: 89).[1] The methodology
that we shall employ breaks from both the Walrasian and the
Marshallian traditions in neoclassical economics, and has a
greater affinity with the Austrian tradition of Carl Menger,
Eugen Böhm-Bawerk and Ludwig von Mises, among others. On
a superficial level, the most noticeable difference between the
Austrian and mainstream approaches is that Austrian analysis
makes much more limited use of mathematical modelling. It is
important to realize, however, that this variance in style is
symptomatic of a more fundamental methodological rift. Upon
reading Walras, Menger sensed a profound difference of
approach which he attempted to discuss with Walras in
correspondence. Jaffé writes:

Carl Menger declared his objection *in principle* to the use of
mathematics as a method of advancing economic knowledge.
He granted that mathematics has its uses as an expository
device and as a subsidiary *Hilfsmittel* but genuine research or
investigation, Menger insisted, should be directed towards
the discovery of the underlying elementary causes of
economic phenomena in all their manifold complexity. For
the performance of this task what is required is not the mathematical method, but a method of process analysis tracing the

complex phenomena of the social economy to the underlying atomistic forces at work.

(Jaffé 1983: 321)

While the focus in the general equilibrium approach is often only on characterizing the equilibrium state, our focus is on a causal representation of the economic processes that lead in the direction of a hypothetical equilibrium (Mises 1949: 353–4). Moreover, we maintain the assumption of equilibrating tendencies in individual markets without the much stronger assumption that the economy as a whole is tending towards a state in which all markets achieve an equilibrium simultaneously. An attempt is made to capture the market processes by rendering empirically plausible causal sequences of events grounded in statements about individual preferences and expectations. The analysis aims to be realistic and to 'portray individuals as deciding and acting in real or historical time, under conditions of genuine uncertainty and change' (O'Driscoll and Rizzo 1986: 252).

Many of the differences between mainstream neoclassical theorizing and what we shall attempt stem from our choice of a causal mode of explanation. It is true that when a mainstream economic model is presented, it is often accompanied with a causal 'story' designed to help the audience better understand it. But the story is regarded as a mere heuristic and not considered respectable science on its own. Our view is just the opposite. A well-developed causal story resting on explicitly stated and empirically justifiable assumptions constitutes the core of an economic theory; and mathematics, if used at all, is employed only as a means towards expositional clarity.

One argument given by general equilibrium theorists for abandoning causal explanations in favour of simultaneous equation models is that in economics everything depends on everything else and that causal chains cannot adequately capture this interdependence. Two responses can be made to this argument. The first is that a causal chain can, indeed, represent interdependence. Take for instance the insight that a 'change in tastes will influence the price of a pound of salmon relative to the price of a pound of calf's liver; [and that] this will influence the quantity produced of certain wines as well as their price' (Duffie and Sonnenschein 1989: 567). One can just as easily derive it employing a causal analysis, as one can employing simultaneous equations. The second response to the interdependence argument is that while everything does depend on everything else, some things will depend more than others. If some factors exert a greater influence than others, then it might be useful to make some attempt to separate out the more significant ones.

Another aspect of our analysis that follows in the Austrian tradition is that we divide our causal theory of the rate of interest into two stages. The first stage is to ask the 'essentialist' question of why positive interest should exist at all. We explore the question in Chapter 3. The second stage, dealt with in Chapter 4, is to ask the more precise question of what causes the interest rate to take on the particular level that we observe. The answer will be seen to require a more detailed look at the market processes in the cash–debt market. It ought to be noted that dividing the analysis into two stages in this way is done for reasons of expositional ease and is not meant to imply that the two questions are unrelated. We agree, as did Böhm-Bawerk ([1912] 1959, 3: 191–2), with Fisher's (1930: 13–14) claim that the 'second question . . . embraces also the first, since to explain how the rate of interest is determined involves the question of whether the rate can or cannot be zero, i.e., whether a positive rate of interest must necessarily exist'.

Before we embark on the two stages, however, it is necessary first to clarify some of the terms that we shall be employing.

LIQUIDITY

Liquidity is a term, like many others found in economics, without a precise and definite meaning. After the stock market plunge of October 19 1987, economists could be heard recommending that the Federal Reserve operate to 'pump liquidity' into the system. On that occasion, liquidity seemed to be used as a euphemism for money: a public partly educated by the monetarist message of the previous decade might have dismissed the advocate of a policy of pumping *money* into the system as inflationist, and substituting the vaguer term liquidity served well to obfuscate the issue. In seeming opposition to this use of the word, financiers use it to refer to a specific quality of assets. Kaufman (1986: 54), for example, writes that liquidity 'means being able to dispose of a financial asset at par, or close to it'.

Among academic economists the term is not used any more

consistently. While there exists an extensive literature, based on Keynes' *General Theory*, in which liquidity is defined clearly as a quantity of money deflated by the price level, other academic economists attach a more elusive meaning to the word. Hicks (1979: 94), for example, writes that 'liquidity is freedom'. In saying so, he echoes Robertson (1940: 32) who equates it with 'freedom of manoeuvre'. And Shackle (1972: 216), working along similar lines, states that liquidity is 'a substitute for knowledge'.

The lack of cohesion evident in the way in which the term liquidity is used justifies, and indeed necessitates, the stipulation of a definition. An attempt will be made to capture as completely as possible the strands of meaning manifested in the statements quoted above. Yet it must be admitted at the outset that any consistent synthesis of such divergent notions must, at some points at least, conflict with accepted usages of the term. Our ultimate goal in stipulating a definition is not to find one that agrees with every sense in which the word has ever been used but rather to discover one on the basis of which a sound liquidity preference theory of interest can be erected.

The redefinition of liquidity represents the first apparent difference between our restatement of the liquidity preference theory of interest and the theory as it is normally interpreted. In conventional textbook interpretations, liquidity means simply a quantity of money deflated by the price level and liquidity preference is represented by the demand function for deflated money. One of the aims of our restatement, however, is to make the theory consistent with the corpus of neoclassical thought which makes the distinction between subjective valuations and the market phenomena to which they give rise. Thus, in our scheme liquidity preference enters as a subjective valuation and the demand for money, deflated or otherwise, will be shown to be, in part, a consequence of that preference.

Under our definition liquidity is a quality that economic decision-makers ascribe to an asset. There are two facets to the liquidity judgment. The first involves an estimate of the transactions costs that might be involved if one were to try to sell the asset. The smaller the expected transactions costs as a proportion of the asset's exchange value the more liquidity will be ascribed to it. The transactions costs of selling an asset reflect the difficulty of locating a buyer willing to pay a high price. One factor that might affect the difficulty is the degree of indivisibility of the asset. A gold brick is more difficult to sell than an equal amount of gold divided into wafers because of the small number of investors seeking to buy that much gold. Another factor affecting the difficulty of selling an asset is the amount of knowledge possessed by potential buyers about the quality of the asset. Suppose I wish to sell a debt issued by a friend. I know my friend is a perfectly reliable borrower but people who do not know him are suspicious. Therefore, in order to get a high price for the debt, I must shoulder the expense of tracking down his other friends.

Besides the asset-holder's expectation of the transactions costs involved in selling the asset, the other, equally important, facet of the liquidity judgment is the degree of certainty with which one holds the estimate of its future value. The more certain economic agents are about how much an asset will be worth in the future, the more liquidity they will ascribe to it. This facet explains why assets with prices fixed in terms of the unit of account are often more liquid than assets with variable unit of account prices. One hundred dollars would probably be considered more liquid than a share of Northern Telecom even if the cost of selling the share was negligible. The reason is that one probably has a greater sense of uncertainty about what the share will be worth in the future than one has about the hundred dollars.

The liquidity judgment is, in essence, an uncertain expectation. A common convention in economics is to employ the mean and variance of a subjective probability distribution as the appropriate representation of an expectation and the uncertainty with which it is held. We shall reject this procedure for the simple reason that it does not seem to accurately reflect what goes through people's minds when they make a liquidity judgment (Hicks 1979: 85). The conventional procedure suggests that when an investor is asked what he thinks his IBM stock will be worth in six months, he admits to being uncertain of the exact value yet at the same time will claim he is sure of the probability that the value will fall within a given range. One could modify the conventional approach by saying the subjective probability distribution is held with uncertainty but we shall take the more straightforward tack of clearing the analysis of subjective probability distributions altogether. The degree of uncertainty attaching to an expectation will be taken to mean the degree of ignorance – both about the correct value and its probability distribution. Keynes' forceful expression of this concept of uncertainty is often quoted:

> The sense in which I am using the term [uncertain knowledge] is that in which the prospect of a European war is uncertain, or the price of copper and the rate of interest twenty years hence, or the obsolescence of a new invention, or the position of private wealth owners in the social system in 1970. About these matters there is no scientific basis on which to form any calculable probability whatever. We simply do not know.
>
> (Keynes [1937] 1973, 14: 113–14)

Writers in finance sometimes make the distinction between liquidity, referring only to the transactions costs of selling an asset, and price risk, referring to the uncertainty about its future value. We are bundling the two concepts together in our definition since the two are often bundled together in the mind of the asset-holder. It is often the case that there are several estimates of the price that an asset will command, with each estimate corresponding to a different transactions cost. The transactions costs involved in selling one's car, for example, would be virtually nil, if one were prepared to accept a low enough price. If one wished to obtain a higher price, it would be necessary to incur higher transactions costs as well. It would make sense that in forming the liquidity judgment, the agent would select the expected price and corresponding expected transactions costs that maximize their difference. It is the difference between them that ends up in his pocket so it is reasonable to suppose the agent would be interested in the maximum value of that amount. Unfortunately, the uncertainty attaching to any investment makes it difficult to do such a computation. A realistic analysis must recognize that the liquidity judgment is unavoidably vague.

LIQUIDITY PREFERENCE

Preference is a relational term so the first question that needs to be addressed in a discussion of liquidity preference is what liquidity is preferred to. The answer is that more liquidity is preferred to less; that is to say, if one is given the choice of two assets equal in all respects except in the amount of liquidity they possess, as a general rule, one will choose the asset possessing the more liquidity. Our liquidity preference theory of interest will claim that this preference has important causal significance in explaining both the level and the existence of the rate of interest. In this section, we explore the meaning of liquidity preference and argue that it is a preference common to most economic decision-makers.

Recall that we have defined liquidity such that an asset will contain more liquidity the smaller are the expected transactions costs as a proportion of the expected exchange value of the asset and the greater is the degree of certainty with which the expectation of the exchange value is held. The reason an asset with low selling costs is preferred *ceteris paribus* to one with higher selling costs is clear. It is a simple example of the familiar feature of economic agents that they prefer more generalized purchasing power to less. The reason they would prefer an asset whose future value is more certain is less obvious.

Assets whose future value is more certain are desirable because they allow one greater scope for planning in the face of an uncertain future. In a world fraught with unexpected emergencies and opportunities, it pays to be prepared. By holding assets about whose realizable value one feels certain, agents have the luxury of knowing that if a sudden emergency occurs, they will be able to cope with it – the precautionary motive; and that if a chance opportunity arises they can grasp it – the speculative motive.[2] In contrast, if agents hold wealth in an asset about whose realizable value they are not certain, then they are prone to the discomfort of knowing that its price might be unusually low at the time when the roof begins to leak or when a hot tip concerning some investment opportunity comes along. In the first case, one might be forced to sell at the unusually low price and in the second, one might have to pass up on the opportunity.

Tobin (1958) isolates risk aversion as the reason for liquidity preference. According to Tobin, people hold liquid assets even when a greater rate of return could be got on illiquid assets because of their fear of the potential capital loss from holding only the latter. While we allow that more than just a fear of capital loss contributes to produce a liquidity preference, and while we reject as unrealistic his assumption that wealth-holders form subjective probability distributions, of the return on various assets, we can still accept the essential idea of Tobin's 1958 paper.

Rather than assuming subjective probability distributions, all we need to suppose is that wealth-holders form some 'guesstimate' of the future value of an asset and have some feeling about how much certainty to attach to it. If, when given a choice between the asset of uncertain value and a sure sum of money smaller than the value of the guesstimate, they choose the latter, then we could say they are risk averse. The reason behind the choice of a sure sum of money smaller than the guesstimate is most likely the very same reason behind the preference for assets about whose value one is more certain, that is, one's desire to be prepared when a contingency arises.

Risk aversion, then, can be viewed as simply another way of expressing the desire to keep one's options open in the face of an uncertain future. In sum, the difference between our explanation of liquidity preference and Tobin's is two-fold. While we agree that risk aversion is a cause of liquidity preference, we differ in adopting a definition of risk aversion that assumes less knowledge on the part of the asset-holder, and allowing that risk aversion is only part of the reason for liquidity preference – the other is a preference for assets with lower selling costs.

Liquidity preference would seem to be a common, and almost universal, choice on the part of asset-holders. An inverted yield curve, however, seems to suggest a preference for the less over the more liquid asset. Take, for example, a situation in which one-year bonds have a yield of 12 per cent and thirty-year bonds have a yield of 10 per cent. Such a situation might arise if people expect interest rates to fall. In a situation of falling interest rates, the thirty-year bond with a yield of 10 per cent seems an attractive investment opportunity and an investor might choose it over a one-year bond paying a higher rate of interest. Given our definition of liquidity, however, a one-year bond appears to be more liquid than a thirty-year bond and in accepting a lower rate of return on the less liquid asset, the investor seems to be indicating a preference for less over more liquidity. In fact, there is no such indication and the paradox arises from not looking at the proper time horizon. It is only in the first year that the strategy of buying the short-term bond is expected to yield more than the strategy of buying the long-term bond. Our investor may believe that over the following years he will be unable to find a bond of any maturity paying as high as 10 per cent. He perceives that over the long-term the purchase of the thirty-year bond will yield a higher rate of return than the strategy of buying a one-year bond and trying to find another investment opportunity at the end of the year. It is not strictly true, then, that in choosing the long-term bond the investor is choosing a lower rate of return. So it is not true that he is demonstrating an illiquidity preference.

There are, however, a couple of cases in which an illiquidity preference might emerge. First, when one is certain about an asset's value, one is guarded against the possibility that its value will be unusually low at an inopportune time; yet by the same token, one is sure that its value will never be unusually high. If an asset-holder has a strong preference for pleasant surprises and likes them more than he or she dislikes unpleasant surprises of an equal magnitude, then there will be a reason to prefer an asset about whose future value there is less certainy. If the effect of this preference outweighs the negative effect of any higher transactions costs involved with the asset whose future value is less certain, then the asset-holder will prefer the illiquid over the liquid asset.

Another reason that one might prefer the illiquid asset is that it can serve as a means of self-restraint. Generally, more options are preferred to fewer and a liquid asset provides the greater number of options. Yet if people have poor self-discipline, they might wish, in a moment of foresight, to limit their options: they might decide to tie up their savings in an illiquid asset simply to avoid the temptation of a short-sighted dissipation.

Despite these two cases of an illiquidity preference, it is reasonable to suppose that as an empirical matter, liquidity preference dominates. While the attraction towards risk and the poor self-discipline that might generate an illiquidity preference are not extremely rare human character traits, they are not necessarily found in those who control most of the economy's wealth.

THE RATE OF INTEREST

For the purposes of our restatement of the liquidity preference theory of interest, we shall define interest as the percentage premium that a borrower pays a lender when exchanging a future claim denominated in the unit of account for a present claim also denominated in the unit of account. Thus, if a borrower exchanges a promise to pay $110 in a year's time for a cheque for

$100 that can be drawn immediately on the lender's bank account, then the percentage premium, or rate of interest, is 10 per cent per annum. We shall be abstracting from term structure and the focus of the analysis will be on the abstraction called 'the' rate of interest. Traditionally, economic theorists have conceived of 'the' rate of interest as being the rate on long-term bonds. We will follow in that tradition. The implicit assumption is that short-term rates of interest are not fundamental; that is, short-term rates can be seen as derivative from long-term rates. We shall accept this assumption as a working hypothesis.

By defining the object of our inquiry as something that arises in the exchange of unit of account denominated claims, we depart from the dualistic treatment of interest in which a hypothetical natural, real, or originary rate of interest is distinguished from the monetary, contractual, or actual rate that we observe. Meta-phorically, the natural rate of interest is understood to be the rate of interest appearing in the real economy that lies beneath the veil of money. Just as physicists, in attempting to understand the real world phenomenon of falling bodies might abstract from air resistance to reach the pure phenomenon of gravity, those with the dualistic vision believe that to understand real world interest rates, they must abstract from money to reach the pure phenomenon of the natural rate of interest. The thinking is that once a theory of the natural rate of interest is developed, the complicating influences of money can then be added to explain what one actually observes.

The distinction between the natural and monetary rate of interest which dates back to the classical economists, may have arisen out of a desire to avoid the fallacies of naive monetary theories of interest. A naive monetary theory of interest might say that interest is determined by the demand and supply of money, just as the price of shoes is determined by their demand and supply. The problem with such a theory is that it implies that an increase in the supply of money will cause a reduction in the interest rate, which is arguably not the case if the increase in the supply of money causes an expectation of an increase in the price level. It is not clear, however, that framing one's theory in terms of a monetary rate of interest necessarily leads one to commit this sort of nominalist fallacy. In fact, it could be argued that abstracting from money carries with it its own dangers. Schumpeter, for instance, warns:

It is true that goods and not 'money' are needed to produce in the technical sense. But if we conclude from this that money is only an intermediate link, merely of technical importance, and set about substituting for it the goods which are obtained with it and for which therefore in the last analysis interest is paid, we at once lose the ground from under our feet. Or more correctly expressed: we can indeed take a step or even a few steps away from the money basis into the world of commodities. But the road suddenly ends because these premiums on commodities are not permanent – and then we see at once that this road was wrong, for an essential characteristic of interest is that it is permanent. Therefore it is impossible to pierce the money veil in order to get the premiums on concrete goods. If one penetrates through it one penetrates into a void.

Thus we cannot move away from the money basis of interest . . . this money form is not shell but kernel.

(Schumpeter [1911] 1961: 184–5)

Another objection to defining the interest rate as the premium arising when future unit of account denominated claims are exchanged for present ones is that the definition seems to suggest interest can arise only in economies with an established unit of account. A more general theory, it could be argued, ought to be able to explain the rate of intertemporal exchange, not just between unit of account denominated claims, but between non-money goods, as well. Our position is somewhat akin to that of a labour economist who restricts himself to explaining money wages even though he realizes that historically, and even today in some places, workers are paid in kind. The justification for restricting the institutional context of the theory to a modern, free market, money-using economy is that such a theory ought to be able to generate richer, more specific results. While stripping one's theory of institutional structure does allow one to draw more general conclusions, the drawback is that the conclusions will be vaguer and without as much content.

Our proposed definition coincides well with most observed forms of interest. An exception, however, is the interest that is earned on certain kinds of present unit of account denominated claims such as Negotiable Order of Withdrawal (NOW) accounts and shares in checkable Money Market Mutual Funds. We have defined interest as a premium arising when a future claim exchanges for a present claim, but in these cases we have a premium arising when one kind of present claim (e.g. a pay cheque) exchanges for another (e.g. a NOW account).

Within our scheme, however, the interest that is paid on these sorts of present claims can be distinguished from interest in the strict sense in which we have defined it. Moreover, one can argue that the interest on present claims is derived from interest in the strict sense. The ability of a financial institution to provide an asset that is payable on demand and yields a positive rate of return relies on its power to pool funds and to exploit the law of large numbers. Consider, for example, current accounts that pay interest. A bank's managers are able to predict with a fair degree of actuarial certainty how much money will be drawn from these deposits on a given day. Only that amount needs to be held in present claims and the rest may be lent out. The money earned on the loans is undoubtedly interest, it is a premium earned for giving up a present claim in exchange for a future claim. Yet when a share of this premium is passed on to the depositors, it ceases to be interest in the strict sense. Rather, it can be interpreted as payment for cooperation in making funds available for lending.

Another form of interest that does not appear to fit well with our proposed definition is the interest on call loans. With a call loan, the borrower issues a promise to pay on a specified date, but unlike an ordinary loan, his promise to pay can be sold back to him at a set price any time before the maturity date. It appears again that we have a case in which interest emerges when one type of present, or immediate, claim exchanges for another. The way out of the seeming inconsistency is to think of a call loan as being made up of two parts: one part is a regular loan in which the borrower sells a future claim in exchange for a present one and the other part is the sale by the borrower of a put option giving the lender the option to sell back the future claim before maturity at a set price. Given this way of thinking about a call loan, the actual interest paid is equal to interest proper minus the price of the put option. In a similar way, we can deal with those loan contracts in which the borrower has the option to pay back the loan any time before maturity. In this case, the actual interest paid is equal to interest proper plus the price of a call option.

Under most circumstances, an interest rate will include a risk premium that compensates the lender for bearing the risk of default. We shall abstract from the risk premium and attempt only to explain the rate of interest on a hypothetical loan completely free from default risk. Bonds issued by stable fiat currency governments come closest to such loans since the governments could conceivably create as much money as was needed to pay off the debtors. In a financial emergency, however, there is no guarantee that they would do so and a small measure of default risk remains. In addition to default risk, we shall also abstract from some other, non-essential influences on the interest rate: we shall abstract from transactions or brokerage costs involved in matching lenders with borrowers that are sometimes incorporated into an interest rate, non-uniform levels of taxation and inflationary premia that participants in the cash–debt market attach to their supply and demand prices.

Traditionally, economists have been concerned with the explanation of the real versus the nominal rate of interest. The real interest rate is defined as the nominal minus the expected, or sometimes the actual, rate of inflation.[3] We find that neither definition is suitable in our version of the liquidity preference theory. If the real rate of interest is defined as the nominal rate minus the actual rate of inflation, then we are explaining the real rate only if all inflation is perfectly foreseen. For our purposes, however, an assumption of perfect foresight is unacceptable since the liquidity preference theory relies on decision-making in an environment of uncertainty to generate its results. If, on the other hand, the real rate of interest is defined as the actual rate minus *the* expectation of inflation, then the question arises of how expectations that are heterogeneous across the population can be reduced to one number. Instead of employing the traditional concept of the real rate of interest, we proceed in the first instance by abstracting from the market participants' inflationary premia, that is, we seek to explain the nominal rate of interest that would exist if the inflationary premia were all zero.

A further difficulty with the traditional concept can be illustrated with an example. Suppose there is a high rate of deflation that is perfectly foreseen – prices are dropping by 50 per cent a year, say. The nominal rate of interest in this case is uncertain but will be greater than zero: someone with money to lend needs an inducement to lend it as opposed to just holding onto it. Let's say the nominal rate is x per cent, where x is greater than zero. The real rate of interest is then $(x + 50)$ per cent. Now, to compare that real rate with the rate of interest that we are analysing, we have to ask ourselves what the nominal rate of interest would be if everything was the same except that there was no expected or actual deflation. Only if we believe the nominal rate would be as high as $(50 + x)$ per cent is our concept equivalent to the traditional real rate of interest. But there's no reason to believe it would be that high.

While it simplifies matters to abstract from the economic agents' inflationary expectations, they are nevertheless a highly volatile and sometimes substantial component of real world interest rates. Once the basic theory is established, therefore, we shall relax the assumption and allow for their influence.

Chapter 3

The theory of interest from an 'essentialist'[1] perspective

We understand the phenomenon if we have recognized the reason for its existence (the reason for its being and so being).
(Carl Menger 1883 (Kauder 1957: 411))

THE 'ESSENTIALIST' PERSPECTIVE

In this chapter, we shall follow what Samuelson (1967: 28) has called 'the old-fashioned methodological procedure' of establishing the *essence* of interest, or of establishing 'why there should (have to) be a positive rate of interest'. The ascendancy of mathematical modelling in mainstream economics has to a large extent eclipsed this kind of question. Within the Austrian school, however, it has a long and continued tradition. In response to Walras's early attempt at a model of a general economic equilibrium, Menger wrote to him asking how the study of mathematical relationships alone can give one knowledge of the 'essence' (*das Wesen*) of economic phenomena (Jaffé 1935: 200). In a similar vein, Mayer (1932), a successor of Menger in the economics chair at the University of Vienna, contrasted the functionalist method of the Lausanne school with the 'causal genetic' method of the Austrians. While the functionalists follow in the footsteps of the physicists in seeking to construct purely mathematical models of the economy, those employing the causal genetic approach attempt to discover the essence, or the originating cause, of the phenomena they study. And, since a statement of causality cannot be expressed mathematically, they are forced to go beyond the limited language of the functionalists.

The opposing perspectives on the methodology of economics are brought out in Böhm-Bawerk's ([1912] 1959, 3: 189–92) discussion of Fisher's theory of interest. Fisher was one of the earliest American economists to employ the general equilibrium method of the Lausanne school and his theory of interest still survives in textbooks today. Böhm-Bawerk, however, educated in the tradition of the Austrian school, could only find in Fisher what seemed to him a 'vicious circle of explanation'. About Fisher's defence of the general equilibrium method, Böhm-Bawerk concludes that it 'reveals very dubious notions on the nature of an explanation to which he was led by his mathematic train of thought and approach'. He goes on to contrast 'mathematical and causal "solutions"' to economic problems and says: 'Mathematical determination is neutral with regard to the question of causality. It has nothing to do with it.' Elaborating, he writes:

Fisher differs from me in that he does not separate his explanation of the *origin* of interest from that of its *rate*. He rejects intentionally and expressly such a separation and limits his presentation to the determining factors of the interest rate. According to him, 'to determine the rate of interest will include the determination of whether the rate must necessarily always be greater than zero'.

Properly understood this is indeed correct. But this method renders a clear elaboration of the sources of interest more difficult, which are by no means identical with the determining factors of its rate. All interest-originating causes undoubtedly are also determining factors for the actual rate. But not all rate-determining factors are also interest-creating causes; they may also be *obstacles* that have been overcome. When we inquire into the causes of a flood we certainly cannot cite the dams and reservoirs built to prevent or at least mitigate inundations. But they are a determining factor for the actual water-mark of the flood. They check the flooding of the river's banks or, in case they cannot prevent this entirely, tend to mitigate the extent of the flood. Similarly, there are other circumstances besides the actual interest-creating causes that bring about or enhance the value advantage of present goods over future goods. There are circumstances that tend inversely to counteract this advantage but are too weak to eliminate it entirely. They undoubtedly are determining factors for the rate of interest, but undoubtedly are not originating causes of it.
(Böhm-Bawerk [1912] 1959, 3: 191–2)

The Austrian concern with originating causes is related to the belief in a fundamental difference between the methods of the social sciences and those of the physical sciences. While they may agree that in the physical sciences the idea of finding originating causes is obsolete, they can maintain that, with the social sciences, the case is different. Ludwig Lachmann, for example, writes:

The idea of Causality falls into the same class of notions discarded by modern natural science, but which the social sciences must retain. The very 'anthropomorphic connotations' which make the concept so suspect in the eyes of modern scientists eager to purge their terminology of anything not 'observable', make it valuable to us. After all, we *are* concerned with the 'anthropomorphic'.

(Lachmann [1950] 1977: 169)

The functionalist perspective, on the other hand, assumes that the methodology of the physical sciences can and should be carried over to the social sciences. This perspective is revealed by Weintraub, a modern expositor and advocate of the general equilibrium approach. He writes:

Once upon a time, science or natural history studied 'causation': What causes the sun to rise? What caused the battle to be lost? What caused the wealth of nations? Explanation of a phenomenon was equivalent to discovery of the cause of that phenomenon. Hume's criticism of the concept of causality, his analysis that suggested that causality could mean no more, but no less, than a relationship between events, led gradually to a different approach to the growth of knowledge. Specifically, the focus of science became 'explanation', and, epistemological issues aside, explanation came to depend on the construction of mathematical arguments in which laws or assumptions entailed conclusions that were potentially falsifiable. The assumptions explained the conclusions; the theory or model explained the phenomena.

(Weintraub 1982: ix)

Although most economists may not be as extreme as Weintraub in claiming that causal explanation no longer has a place in economics, looking through leading academic journals, one can conclude the functionalist perspective is now dominant. In this chapter, we reopen the debate among interest rate theorists that raged in the early part of the century (see Seager 1912; Brown 1913, 1914; Fetter [1914] 1977), but which was never resolved. Rather, it was quieted, as Fisher's (1907, 1930) simultaneous equation mode of explanation took centre stage and rendered moot the essentialist question of originating causes. In reopening the debate at this later date, we are able to extend it by incorporating voices that were not heard from earlier. In addition to considering the traditional candidates of impatience and the productivity of capital, we bring attention to the thesis propounded by Schumpeter in his *Theory of Economic Development* ([1911] 1961) that it is the expectation of super-normal profits that explains the existence of positive interest; and to the idea presented in rather embryonic form by Keynes (1936) that liquidity preference is the explanation.

The way we shall proceed is to consider various elements that come into play in the money loan market where the interest rate appears and to ask ourselves which of these elements could be construed as originating causes. To this end we begin by asking about each factor X: Could X exist without interest existing? If the answer is yes, a world is conceivable in which X is present but interest is not, then we eliminate X as a candidate for being an originating cause. If, however, the factor passes this test and it is determined that whenever X exists, interest also exists, then we ask the additional question of whether the causality might run from interest to X. If it becomes clear that it is more reasonable to suppose that X is caused by interest than the other way around, then again X is rejected as the originating cause.

The analysis in this chapter carries with it the limitation that it cannot establish for certain what is the originating cause of interest: it can only claim to establish what is not. In the concluding section we will say more about this limitation and the way it might be overcome. We now examine the following candidates and ask about each of them if they might be the originating cause of interest: (1) the productivity of capital defined in three different ways, (2) the preference for present over future consumption, and (3) liquidity preference.

THE PRODUCTIVITY OF CAPITAL

The productivity of capital has long been considered a causal factor in the explanation of the interest rate. In this section we ask if it can be considered an originating cause: that is, we ask if the alleged productivity of capital furnishes a reason for the existence of interest. We look at three different interpretations of the term. The first, which we shall call the physical productivity of capital, corresponds to those situations in which the capital-using[2] method of production yields more output per unit of input than the non-capital using method. If, with his endowment of labour time, Crusoe can catch more fish with a net that he constructs himself than if he catches them directly by hand, then we can say the net-using, or more capitalistic, method of production is physically more productive. The second interpretation can be labelled the value productivity of capital and it simply corresponds to those situations in which the value of the output of a capitalistic method of production is greater than the value of the inputs.

These two interpretations of the productivity of capital are the most common ones. For the sake of completeness, however, we shall consider a third, quite different, interpretation. We shall call it the expected super-productivity of capital and it will be said to be evident when an entrepreneur believes that by investing in a particular capitalistic method of production he can reap a super-normal rate of return. Schumpeter in his *Theory of Economic Development* ([1911] 1961) was the first to propound the novel thesis that this expectation of super-normal profits was the originating cause of interest.

To begin with, consider the hypothesis that the physical productivity of capital is the reason for the existence of a positive rate of interest. As a means of evaluating this hypothesis we ask if a world is conceivable in which capital is productive in this physical sense but in which the rate of interest is zero. The physical productivity of capital is most clearly evident in those examples in which the input and the output of the production process are the same good but in which more of the output can be produced simply by waiting longer: one can think of Ricardo's corn, Fisher's sheep, or Samuelson's rice. In Samuelson's (1981: 22) example, one bushel of rice this year ripens into one and a tenth bushels next year. The question we want to ask is whether this technological fact is reason for a present claim denominated in the unit of account to exchange at a premium with a future claim denominated in the unit of account.

If the price of rice in terms of the unit of account is constant through time, then in Samuelson's example, a 10 per cent rate of interest on unit of account denominated loans represents an equilibrium. If the rate of interest were less, there would be an incentive to borrow and invest in present rice, driving the price of future rice down and the interest rate and the price of present rice up. If the rate of interest were greater than 10 per cent, there would be an incentive to sell today's rice and lend the money out, driving the price of future rice up and the interest rate and the price of present rice down. Yet although a 10 per cent rate of interest represents an equilibrium when the price of rice is constant in terms of the unit of account, there is no reason for us to expect a constant price. There is nothing inconsistent about a world in which one bushel of rice ripens into one and a tenth bushels and in which the price of rice in both real terms and in terms of the unit of account falls by approximately 9.1 per cent each year. In this world, the equilibrium interest rate (real and nominal) is zero. It is conceivable, then, for physically productive capital to co-exist with a zero rate of interest and we are led, on the basis of our first criterion, to reject the physical productivity of capital as an explanation of why the interest rate is positive.

In the first volume of his *Capital and Interest*, Böhm-Bawerk presents a comprehensive critique of theories that attribute the existence of interest to the productivity of capital. He shows that either theorists have neglected to demonstrate that physical productivity leads to the existence of surplus value or that they have tried and failed. Yet in the second volume, Böhm-Bawerk claims that the technical superiority of present goods is a reason they are valued higher than future goods – that is, their technical superiority is responsible for the existence of interest. His second volume's recognition of physical productivity as an originating cause of interest has been considered by Fetter ([1902] 1977: 185) and others to be a surprising reversion.

There is a difference, however, between Böhm-Bawerk's theory and the ones he was criticizing. The difference he made to the debate was to frame the argument not in terms of some elusive substance 'capital' but rather in terms of concrete present and future goods. '*Present goods are as a general rule worth more than future goods of equal quality and quantity*. That sentence is the nub and kernel of the theory of interest which I have to present' (Böhm-Bawerk [1912] 1959, 2: 259). Böhm-Bawerk terms this divergence in value 'originary interest' and maintains that originary interest is the cause of interest on unit of account de-nominated loans. He writes: 'The matter calling for explanation is originary interest. Now there is no question that contract interest (loan interest) is founded in all essential respects on originary interest, and can be easily dealt with in a secondary explanation, once originary interest has been satisfactorily explained' ([1914] 1959, 1: 76).

For the case in which the input and the output of the time consuming process are the same good, the truth of Böhm-Bawerk's contention that physical productivity is a sufficient condition for originary interest is easily established. If a bushel of 1988 rice ripens into a bushel and a tenth of 1989 rice, then only the assumption of non-satiation (or alternatively free disposal) is necessary to establish that a bushel of 1988 rice is worth more than a bushel of 1989 rice. With a bushel of 1988 rice, I can enjoy it now or enjoy 1.1 bushels in 1989. With a bushel of 1989 rice, there is no possibility of enjoying it in the present; rather, I must wait and end up with less rice than if I had chosen the 1988 bushel.

Yet the criticism presented above of the notion that physical productivity can serve as the originating cause of loan interest still stands. The fact that a bushel of 1988 rice is worth more than a bushel of 1989 rice is not reason for anyone to agree to pay positive interest on a unit of account denominated loan, as we have demonstrated above in the example in which the price of rice was falling. Thus our quarrel with Böhm-Bawerk is not that he is wrong to identify the technical superiority of present goods as a reason for the existence of what he calls originary interest but rather that he fails to demonstrate that his originary interest is a reason for the existence of loan interest.

Fisher (1930: 194) maintains that if the rate of transformation between present goods and future goods was fixed, that is, if the production possibility frontier was a straight line, then the rate of interest would be determined by the physical productivity. To this extent, he was a pure physical productivity theorist. Our objection to his analysis parallels our objection to Böhm-Bawerk. He gives reason for the rate of exchange between present and future goods to be such that more future goods must be given up for a given number of present goods, yet he does not supply any argument why this fact should necessitate a positive rate of loan interest. To buy one bushel of rice today, I may have to promise a bushel and a tenth next year. Yet that is not to say that to secure $10 today I must promise $11 next year.

Yeager (1979) presents a more extreme version of Fisher's argument by postulating the existence of a machine that transforms any present good into 1.5 future goods. He argues that in such a world the interest rate could not be less than 50 per cent. If he means to include the money good in the goods that can be so transformed then his conclusion is correct. Yet one has reason to question the relevance of his example to the real world. Experience has shown that the good that evolves to serve as money tends to be one that is durable and in fairly constant supply, that is, one that is not readily produced. One might expect that if Yeager's machine came into existence, people would look for something that could not be put into it to serve as money. Moreover, a machine that reproduces money is not what one usually has in mind when one is discussing the productive power of capital. But Yeager's result that the physical productivity of capital determines the interest rate relies on this unusual way of construing the productivity of capital.

We now turn to the second interpretation of the argument that the productivity of capital is the originating cause of interest. This interpretation says that interest exists because of the value productivity of capital; that is, interest exists because by investing a given number of dollars in a capitalistic process of production, one is able to obtain a greater number of dollars at the end of it. The suspicious thing about this argument is that it attempts to explain the value of one thing by the value of another. It is reminiscent of the attempts by the early classical economists to explain the price of a good by adding up the prices of the factors of production that cooperated to produce it. The problem arises when one asks what determines the prices of the factors of production. Some reflection reveals that the price of the good must have some effect on the prices of the factors of production and one ends up reasoning in circles: the price of the good is caused by the prices of the factors and the prices of the factors are caused by the price of the good.

One might argue that the above does not demonstrate circular reasoning but rather is merely the expression of the mutual determination of prices. This line of argument, however, is at odds with our 'essentialist' approach to the problem. We support the view expressed by Menger:

That the parts of a whole and the whole itself can be at once the cause and effect of one another (i.e. that there is mutual determination) which is a point of view that has gained ground . . . is an idea so obscure and inadequate to our laws of thought that we can hardly be wrong in taking it as a sign that our age still lacks in many respects a profound understanding both of natural organisms and of social phenomena.

(Menger [1883] 1963: 144)

In looking for the originating cause of some economic phenomenon, the essentialist is looking for something that does not in turn depend on the phenomenon. If it can be shown, then, that the value productivity depends on the rate of interest, it does not qualify as an originating cause.

We might first ask ourselves how it is that value productivity arises. It cannot be taken by the economist as an exogenous factor because value is something that it is his job to explain. To investigate how it arises, we could consider the straightforward example of two production processes that use identical inputs and differ only in the amount of time it takes for the output to be ready for market. We could consider, for instance, the production of wine that is aged ten years versus a wine that is drunk young. If capital has value productivity then it will be the case that the aged wine will sell for more than the young wine. Economic theory tells us that the value of a good is related to its marginal rate of substitution which is in turn related to its scarcity. Suppose that at the same margin the young and old wines are equally desirable. It follows that the old wine must be produced in quantities such that its marginal rate of substitution is above the marginal rate of substitution of new wine. Since the inputs to both the production processes are the same, one cannot attribute the relative scarcity of the old wine to the scarcity of the factors of production. It turns out that its relative scarcity is actually man-made: it follows from the decisions of how much wine to age. When we look to the individuals making these decisions, we find that they are unwilling to invest in wine that needs to be aged unless they can sell it for a price above that of the new wine. The reason is that they are incurring an opportunity cost: by buying the inputs now and waiting later for the receipts, they are tying up funds that alternatively could be lent out at interest. If too much old wine comes on the market, some wine-makers will find they are making losses in old wine and cut back; if too little is produced, some will find they are making super-normal profits and increase production. The market process leads to the production of the quantity of old wine that causes the value productivity of wine stocks to be equal to the interest rate.

The example above shows that the interest rate influences the entrepreneurs' decisions about how much to produce. These decisions, in turn, determine the prices in which the value productivity of capital is reflected. The interest rate is seen to be crucial in explaining the value productivity of capital. Thus, on the basis of our second criterion, the value productivity of capital cannot be regarded as the originating cause of interest.

Turn now to the third and last of our interpretations of the productivity of capital. We have termed it the expected super-productivity of capital and it corresponds to the expectations on the part of innovative entrepreneurs that they will be able to earn a greater than normal rate of return in their capitalistic ventures. Unlike the physical and value productivity of capital, it is clearly a subjective factor. We might note that the hypothesis that it is a subjective, expectational variable that is the originating cause of interest is consistent with our stated methodological goal of grounding our theory in statements about individual preferences and expectations.

If, in a competitive environment, the value of an output is greater than the value of the inputs that went to produce it, then we would expect production of the output to be expanded until the surplus is driven to zero. Yet this market process can only be expected to happen for known products and techniques. If the economy is in a state of flux with new products and techniques constantly being discovered by entrepreneurs expecting a super-normal rate of return, then it is possible that the surplus will never be driven to zero. It is on this basis that one can argue as Schumpeter ([1911] 1961) did, that the expected super-productivity of capital is the originating cause of interest.

Applying our two criteria for an originating cause, we first ask if it is possible for the expected super-productivity to exist without there being a positive rate of interest. To answer this question we abstract from the other candidates for originating cause: that is to say, we assume people are indifferent both between present and future consumption and between holding their savings in present or future unit of account denominated claims. Given the above assumptions, we would expect a tendency for the value of the inputs of round-about or capitalistic methods of production to match the value of the outputs. If it is the case, however, that at any point in time a set of entrepreneurs exists who are capable of arranging inputs in new ways so that their value is exceeded by the value of the output, then the equilibrating process will never be able to erode away the surplus. A money-lender will charge a positive rate of interest to any borrower because he knows he could always get a positive rate of interest from an innovative entrepreneur.

One qualification is important, though: in order that the expected super-productivity of capital translates into a positive rate of interest, it must be the case that those with the expectation are the same as those with the money capital. An impecunious entrepreneur might expect his invention to reap super-normal profits but those with money to lend may not be so certain. In such a case the expected super-productivity of capital is not sufficient. Given this one qualification, then, the factor passes the first criterion for an originating cause; it is not possible for the expected super-productivity of capital to exist without there being a positive rate of interest.

The second criterion that a factor must pass if it is to be construed as an originating cause of interest is that it is not itself a result of interest. The expected super-productivity of capital is a subjective variable that only relies on the ability of entrepreneurs to discover a more profitable than hitherto way of arranging inputs. As such it can exist no matter what the interest rate. Thus, on both our criteria for an originating cause, the expected super-productivity of capital is unrefuted.

In summary, we have examined three different interpretations of the vague term productivity of capital and have asked of each of them if they might be the originating cause of interest. The physical productivity we discovered fails the first criterion for an originating cause, while the value productivity fails the second. Only the subjective factor that we have labelled the expected super-productivity of capital passes both criteria and thus is the only one to remain as a candidate for originating cause.

THE PREFERENCE FOR PRESENT OVER FUTURE CONSUMPTION

The most difficult task that must be faced in examining the question of whether the preference for present over future consumption could be the originating cause of interest is working out what this preference means. One issue that is raised can be illustrated by means of an example. Suppose a man living in New Jersey spends his entire income and in addition borrows money at the going rate of interest to purchase a car. Suppose further that he has a twin brother of identical means who lives in Manhattan. Both brothers enjoy exactly the same consumption bundle with the exception that the brother who lives in Manhattan spends on taxis, buses and the occasional car rental what his New Jersey twin spends in car payments. Comparing the two brothers, we find that the New Jersey brother is a net borrower at the going rate of interest, while the Manhattan one breaks even. The question is: would we want to characterize the New Jersey brother as having a higher degree of preference for present over future consumption than his Manhattan twin?

Since their consumption patterns are identical except in the way in which their transportation services are obtained, a reasonable use of language would allow one to say that their degree of preference for present over future consumption is the same. Thus, when detecting the degree of time preference, one cannot look just at one's level of spending in any given period because part of that spending might be on consumer durables. In the month that he bought the car, the New Jersey brother perhaps spent $13,000 while his Manhattan twin spent only $3,000. If that extra $10,000 had been dissipated in a trip to Atlantic City, one might be inclined to attribute to him a greater degree of preference for present consumption. But since it went to purchase a good that will yield a flow of consumer services into the future, the interpretation is different.

The decision on the part of the consumer to buy a consumer durable and his willingness to pay interest to do so is analogous to the producer's decision to pay interest to buy a durable producer's good. This type of consumer demand can no more be made the originating cause of interest than the analogous form of producer's demand. The argument that was presented in the previous section as to why the value productivity of capital cannot be the originating cause of interest can be carried over to this case. The consumer is willing to pay positive interest because the value of the flow of services yielded by the consumer good is greater than its current price. Yet this discrepancy in value is properly regarded as the consequence of interest, and thus cannot, without circularity, be regarded as its cause.

In this section we wish to be able to make the distinction between spending current income on durables that represent future enjoyments and spending current income on immediate enjoyments. In order to do so we will consider the preference for present over future consumption to be manifested in the preference for present over future consumption services, rather than in the preference for present over future goods. Under this interpretation a consumption good represents a flow of consumption services, the more durable the good the longer the flow. This is the approach taken by Fisher (1930: 66) in his elucidation of what he calls impatience. It should be noted, however, that in interest theory based on some of the insights of Böhm-Bawerk's *Positive Theory of Capital* ([1912] 1959), the distinction is not made and the analysis is framed purely in terms of a preference for present over future goods. Followers of this approach include Fetter (1904, [1914] 1977) and Mises (1949).

A further reason for adopting the Fisher approach of defining time preference specifically in terms of consumption services, rather than goods, can be illustrated by means of another example. Suppose a woman spends half her income on the necessities of life and spends the other half on gold bullion which she stores away in her safety deposit box. Suppose further she has a twin sister of identical means who also spends half her income on the bare necessities but then spends the other half on theatre tickets and meals at expensive restaurants. Both spend the same amount on present goods; so if one is employing a concept of time preference in which it is equated with the preference for present over future goods, one cannot say whether one sister has a higher degree of time preference than the other. In other words, one is unable to assert that someone who saves half her income has a different degree of time preference than someone who saves nothing, if it happens that her saving is done through the purchase of assets that fall under the category of goods.

In his section on the first cause of interest, Böhm-Bawerk

admits as much when he writes:

> there are very many persons whose present is better provided
> for than is their future, but who enjoy the possibility, not only
> of storing up present goods for the service of the future, but
> also of using them in the interim as a reserve fund. Such
> persons will value present goods as highly as future goods, or
> they will . . . consider them of slightly higher value.
>
> (Böhm-Bawerk [1912] 1959, 2: 268)

In this passage, Böhm-Bawerk reveals that part of the reason
he believes present goods are valued higher than future goods is
that by holding them, one is able to keep them as a reserve fund,
that is, as a liquid store of wealth. If, when the woman visits her
bullion dealer, she is given the option of either getting her gold
immediately or having it delivered in a year's time, she would
most likely choose to get it right away. Her reason for preferring
present gold over future gold is that within the next year an
unexpected opportunity or emergency might arise for which she
would want to sell her gold. If she is holding only a claim to
future gold, it would be more difficult to do so.

Thus, in his exposition of the first cause of interest, Böhm-
Bawerk bundles together two quite different reasons for
preferring present goods over future goods: one is what we are
calling the preference for present over future consumption
relating it to the preference for consumption services that are
immediately enjoyed, and the other is closer to what we define in
the previous chapter as liquidity preference, that is, the
preference to hold assets that expand one's range of options over
assets that are more limiting. Our reason for unbundling these
two reasons for preferring present goods is that we wish to
investigate which is the stronger contender as the originating
cause of interest.

Having specified the object of the preference discussed in this
section as consumption services rather than consumption goods
as such, the next task is to fix on a reasonable interpretation of the
term preference. Generally when economists say that A is preferred to B, they imply that if A and B were to cost the same, A
would be chosen. If an apple and a banana both cost 50 cents and
I choose to buy an apple, one might say I prefer apples. Yet this
conclusion is not so clear when the additional bit of information
that I have just consumed five bananas, is revealed. In a strict

analysis, one can only make a statement about preference at the margin.

The problem of knowing the correct margin is revealed when we consider that if one is enjoying ample consumption in the present and foresees a future time at which one will have nothing, one will be bound to put a higher value on future consumption services; yet if the same person is then impoverished in the present and promised to be well provided for in the future, the preference will be reversed. We are faced, then, with an important question when asking if the preference for present consumption is the originating cause of interest. The question is: at what margin is the preference supposed to exist (Pellengahr 1986)?

A second difficulty in interpreting the concept of a preference for present over future consumption is knowing what point in time to take as the reference point. Suppose the price of consumption is constant through time and we observe someone consuming a great deal in period t – more than he consumed in period $t-1$ and more than he will consume in period $t+1$. The question is whether this consumption pattern is evidence that he prefers consumption in t over consumption in $t+1$ (i.e. that he prefers present over future consumption), or whether it is evidence that he prefers consumption in t over consumption in $t-1$ (i.e., that he prefers future over present consumption). The problem is that future consumption becomes present consumption with the passage of time; so unless a steadily decreasing level of consumption is revealed, one cannot be sure that a preference for present consumption is evident.

In summary, there are two difficulties that must be faced in interpreting a preference for present over future consumption. The first is the problem of knowing the appropriate margin and the second is the problem of knowing the appropriate time reference. In this section we wish to construct an example of a world in which the preference definitely exists and ask whether, in such a world, interest will also exist. Yet in constructing the example, we must find an interpretation of this preference that deals with the two difficulties in a reasonable way.

The interpretation we shall take is to say that if, when the trade-off between present and future consumption is one-for-one, people choose to arrange life-time consumption patterns so that they spend the most when they are young and taper off as they get older, then they exhibit a preference for present over future consumption. It is reasonable to take the relevant margin to be the point at which consumption in the present is equal to consumption in the future. Under our interpretation present consumption is preferred to future at this margin: if one arranges consumption so that one always consumes less in the future than in the present, then at the margin at which one is consuming the same, present consumption must be preferred. Our definition of time preference is consistent with the one proposed by Blaug (1985: 502). He writes that 'to avoid fatal ambiguity of language, we must define "time preference" in terms of a zero rate of interest. Positive time preference means that individuals prefer present income over the same amount of future income despite the fact that these are available on the same terms.'

The difficulty of knowing the appropriate time reference is obviated by our considering the agent's life-time consumption pattern and imposing the condition that the consumption level falls in each period. It ought to be noted that our interpretation of the preference for present over future consumption goes only as far as postulating a sufficient condition for the existence of that preference; it does not pretend to provide the necessary conditions. In other words, we are claiming that a preference for present over future consumption exists if, when the trade-off between present and future consumption is one-for-one, one consumes less in each successive period; but we are not claiming that the preference exists *only* when this condition is satisfied. It is possible that a weaker condition might be consistent with the preference. We are not concerned with capturing the necessary conditions here because they do not serve our ultimate purpose, which is to characterize a world in which the preference for present consumption undoubtedly exists and to ask whether in such a world, interest must also exist.

To say that the preference for present consumption is the originating cause of interest is to say that the demand for present consumption generated by this preference is so high that the loan market will only clear at a positive rate of interest. In other words, if we lived in a world in which loans were only made in order to finance the enjoyment of present consumption services at the expense of future consumption services, that is, if we abstract from loans made for the purpose of buying consumer and producer durables, then the loan market would only clear at a positive rate of interest.

Give the hypothesis its strongest chance and suppose everyone prefers present over future consumption: that is, if the interest rate were zero everyone would operate so as to consume the most when they were young, tapering off as they got older. We investigate the question of whether this type of preference will give rise to positive interest by constructing an example in which there are no consumer or producer durables and in which people are indifferent between holding their savings in dollars and holding them in promises that a reliable borrower will pay them dollars at a mutually agreed point in the future. We suppose there are three generations: the young, the middle-aged and the old. The young earn an income and in addition borrow for current consumption; the middle-aged earn an income which they spend on current consumption, on paying back their loans, and on saving for their old age; and the old earn no income and spend down their savings. The question is whether in this hypothetical world interest is necessary. The answer, we find, is no, interest will not necessarily exist. Interest, if it is to arise at all, emerges in the loans that the middle-aged make to the young. Now, if the amount of wealth that the middle-aged are willing to save at a zero interest rate is equal to or exceeds the amount of wealth that the young wish to borrow at a zero interest rate and if the middle-aged are indifferent between holding their savings in money or bonds, then market forces will eliminate any positive interest.

To sum up, we have examined the question of whether the preference for present over future consumption services might be the originating cause of interest. We have focussed on consumption services rather than the goods that render these services, in order to isolate only the motive of preference for present consumption. The conclusion is that this preference will not generate interest unless it is the case that at a zero rate of interest the demand for loans to finance current consumption is greater than the amount being saved.

At historically experienced interest rates, the demand for loans for current consumption has represented only a tiny fraction of total savings. Asking what would happen at a zero rate of interest requires some speculation but two considerations lead to the conclusion that borrowing for current consumption would probably not exceed savings. The first is that saving is generally done to provide a certain level of income in one's old age. The implication is that a lower interest rate will not cause significantly less saving; in fact, it may cause more, because without interest people have to put away greater amounts to insure the same level of retirement income. The second consideration is that even at a zero interest rate, more borrowing in the present does entail a cost to the consumer – it means less consumption in the future. The situation is not analogous to asking what will be the demand for apples when their price in terms of oranges is zero but rather is analogous to asking what will be the demand for apples when one apple exchanges for one orange. Although there may be more consumer borrowing at a zero interest rate than at a positive rate, the quantity demanded would not balloon as if present consumption were free. Given these two considerations, it seems unlikely that at a zero rate of interest the amount of consumer borrowing would exceed the amount of savings. The conclusion, then, is that the preference for present over future consumption is not a plausible candidate for the originating cause of interest.

It might be argued that the preference for present over future consumption, as we have defined it, is not the originating cause of a positive rate of interest, but that there is an alternative definition under which it is a serious candidate. Mises's (1949) concept of 'time preference', for instance, is clearly different from what we have called a preference for present over future consumption. Time preference, according to Mises, is evident in every act of consumption: the mere fact that I eat lunch today is evidence of time preference. In fact, Mises goes even further in saying that time preference is evident any time I act. The implication is that even if I never eat lunch and instead save my dollars for some future feast, I am still exhibiting time preference.

The core of Mises' theory of interest is found in the following quotations:

> It has been shown that time preference is a category inherent in every human action. Time preference manifests itself in the phenomenon of originary interest, i.e., the discount of future as against present goods.
>
> (Mises 1949: 521)

> Originary interest is the ratio of the value assigned to want-satisfaction in the immediate future and the value assigned to want-satisfaction in remoter periods of the future. It manifests itself in the market economy in the discount of future goods as

against present goods. It is a ratio of commodity prices, not a price in itself. There prevails a tendency toward the equalization of this ratio for all commodities. In the imaginary construction of the evenly rotating economy the rate of originary interest is the same for all commodities.

(Mises 1949: 523)

In saying (1) that time preference is inherent in every human action and (2) that time preference manifests itself in originary interest, he is saying that no matter how people act, originary interest will appear. Originary interest is independent of the kind of action performed. A question that Mises does not address, however, is whether this originary interest will always be positive. If originary interest can be negative then he is not asserting that his 'time preference' is the reason for a positive rate of interest and his discussion is irrelevant to the question being explored in this section.

If, on the other hand, he does believe that originary interest is always positive, then we are left to wonder how any kind of action can give rise to it. Mises states that originary interest 'manifests' itself in the market economy in the discount of future goods as against present goods. Yet he gives no indication how this category, inherent in any human action, is linked to the specific market phenomenon of originary interest.

Moreover, it is not clear from Mises' discussion how he would answer a simple counter-example in which reasonable human action leads to a premium on future goods instead of a discount. Suppose one lives on an island where the only means of sustenance is fresh fish. In this situation, it is possible that to ensure that one has enough to eat when one is old and unfit to catch to fish, one would contract with younger island dwellers to supply future fish in exchange for present fish. In this example, it is conceivable that more present fish will exchange for fewer future fish.

In sum, the first problem posed by the claim that Mises was presenting an alternative candidate for the originating cause of positive interest is knowing whether Mises believed that time preference did, in fact, give rise to positive interest. If he did not, then his theory cannot be taken as constituting a hypothesis about why a positive rate of interest is observed. If he did, however, a second problem emerges. That problem is in knowing how something so general that it is inherent in every human action can give rise to something as specific as the discount on future goods as against present goods.

LIQUIDITY PREFERENCE

All the essentialist explanations for interest that we have been considering in this chapter are time preference theories in the sense that they all assert that interest exists because a present dollar is preferred to a future dollar. Where the explanations part company, however, is in what they assert to be the crucial, or essential, motive behind this preference. In the previous two sections, we considered the motive of wanting to reap the surplus rendered by capitalistic processes of production and the motive Fisher called 'impatience', that is, the desire to enjoy consumption services sooner rather than later. In this section, the motive under investigation is the preference for more over less liquidity. The claim we wish to examine is that one can prefer a dollar today over a promise of a dollar next year, not because one wants to consume now rather than next year, nor because one wants to invest in some kind of productive enterprise. Rather, one can prefer a dollar today simply because one values liquidity: that is, prefers to be more over less certain about the purchasing power of one's assets and likes to know that in the event that one wanted to effect an exchange, it could be done with the minimum of transactions costs.

Interest comes into existence when a future claim denominated in the unit of account (a bond of some sort) is exchanged for a present claim denominated in the unit of account (for example, a cheque or currency). Interest is the premium that the seller of the future claim pays the seller of the present claim. It is easily established that a present claim has more liquidity than a future claim to the same amount. First, the transactions cost of transforming a future claim into immediate purchasing power is higher than for a present claim. While the bearer of a future claim must first find someone to whom he can sell it, the bearer of a present claim is, in most cases, already holding immediate purchasing power. Secondly, the present claim's value in terms of the unit of account is fixed, with the result that one can feel more certain about its purchasing power than one can about a future claim which, before its redemption date, has a variable unit of account price.

If it is true that a present unit of account denominated claim has more liquidity than a future unit of account denominated claim, and that assets with more liquidity are preferred to assets with less, then it follows that a premium must be paid to get one to give up a present unit of account denominated claim in exchange for a future one. The assumption of liquidity preference alone is enough to generate a positive rate of interest. We can conclude, then, that in conformity with our first criterion for an originating cause, it is not possible for liquidity preference to exist without there being a positive rate of interest.

The second criterion says that the candidate for originating cause cannot itself be the result of interest. Keynes' liquidity preference theory was criticized on this ground when it was accused of involving a bootstrap argument (Hicks 1939: 164; Robertson 1940: 25). Keynes' emphasis on the speculative motive led his critics to respond that explaining the existence of interest by reference to the fact that people wish to hold present claims in speculation of an increase in the interest rate, presupposes a positive rate of interest. If there were no interest to begin with, there would be nothing to speculate about and thus no liquidity preference. Keynes' critics were essentialists at heart in intuiting that if one wants to get at the originating cause of interest, one must find something that can exist independently of it.

Two responses can be made to the bootstrap allegation. The simple response is that a liquid asset can be preferred to an illiquid one because it is less costly to transform it into immediate purchasing power and that this aspect of liquidity preference is independent of interest. The other, more subtle but probably more important, response is that the speculative motive lying behind the preference for liquidity depends not on there being interest but in there being an expectation of interest. In a causal analysis, it is important to distinguish between the expectation of a thing and the thing itself. For example, if I decide to carry an umbrella in expectation of rain, one cannot accurately claim that the rain motivated my decision – especially when one considers that it may not rain after all.

A further illustration can be provided by considering how an interest rate might have been determined before there were organized money markets. As Fetter (1904) has argued, interest in one of its earliest forms, after the strictures of the Middle Ages, arose in the purchase and sale of rent charges dating back to the twelfth century. A rent charge is a contract whereby the buyer is given the right to a portion of the rents from a property owned by the seller. The contract provides a property owner with a way to raise a large sum of money. These rent charges were sold for less than the sum of the rent payments, suggesting a rate of discount that can be interpreted as the rate of interest. Now suppose that at a time before these rent charges were common, a country squire amasses a large gambling debt that he is obliged to pay off immediately. His liquid assets are insufficient to cover it so he attempts to sell one of the first rent charges. He approaches the local miser who is reputed to have a hoard of gold coins hidden away and explains the nature of the contract. The question we wish to investigate is what would determine the rate of discount that would persuade the miser to give up his gold.

The miser's first consideration would probably be the liquidity of the rent charge. Although he had not intended to spend down his wealth, some unforeseen event might arise in which he would have to. Before deciding on a rate of discount, therefore, he would want to work out (1) the transactions costs involved in selling the rent charge and (2) what kind of price he could expect to get for it. It is when he thinks about its expected price that he is forced to form an expectation of the interest rate: he must form an expectation of the rate of discount that a secondary buyer would apply to the rent charge. We see, then, that even before the first interest contract is signed, an expectation of a future rate of interest can influence the rate of interest that will emerge. We see that to have the rate of interest depend on the expectation of a future rate breaks no rule of logic and the liquidity preference hypothesis is not vulnerable to the bootstrap allegation.

In our discussion of the preference for present over future consumption, the question of the relevant margin arose. We argued that if we found someone who preferred present over future consumption and then proceeded to arrange that he or she would be less well provided in the future, we could reverse their preference. It turns out that whether one prefers present to future consumption depends on how well endowed one is at different times: that is to say, it depends on the margin from which one is making the choice. We are led to wonder if the same problem of knowing the appropriate margin plagues the liquidity preference explanation of interest. Happily, it does not. If one is going to prefer the more liquid asset, one will do so at all margins. The reason is that the more liquid asset provides one with a greater range of options than the less liquid one. With a dollar today, one can do everything one can do with a promise of a dollar next year (all one needs to do is to hold it a year, at which point the two assets are equivalent) and, one can do more. Within the coming year the present dollar can buy a dollar's worth of goods. But to purchase goods with the promise of a future dollar, one must first find a buyer for the promise. Locating a buyer involves a cost and because the buyer can never be as certain about a promise as about the thing itself, will quite likely only agree to buy it at a discount. The result is that in the coming year, the promise of a future dollar will buy less than a present dollar and the present dollar will be preferred.

As we remarked above, Böhm-Bawerk identifies the motive that we are calling liquidity preference as part of the reason present goods are preferred to future goods. He writes:

> Most goods are durable, especially money, which with its aspect of non-particularization is capable of representing all classes of goods; hence they can be reserved for the service of the future. The situation then, as between present and future goods, is as follows. Future goods are of course adaptable only to future uses. Present goods are adaptable to *those same* future uses, and in addition to present ones or optionally to those other future uses for which opportunity may arise in the interval between the present time and the future period under consideration.
>
> (Böhm-Bawerk [1912] 1959, 2: 266–7)

Yet despite this patch of agreement between Böhm-Bawerk's essentialist explanation and the one we are considering in this section, they are very much at odds with one another. In a nutshell, Böhm-Bawerk's thesis is this: (1) Present goods are preferred to future goods; these goods include money but include other goods as well. (2) The preference for present goods is explained by three causes. (3) Liquidity preference enters as only one part of one of the three causes. (4) The premium generated when present goods exchange for future goods is originary interest and originary interest is the cause of interest on unit of account denominated loans. In contrast, the thesis considered here says: (1) the premium on unit account denominated loans might be caused by liquidity preference alone and (2) that liquidity preference explains loan interest directly so that the postulation of an originary rate of interest is unnecessary.

CONCLUSION

The aim of this chapter has been to investigate the essence of interest. We have interpreted essence to mean the originating cause and have asserted that two criteria must be satisfied if a factor is to be an originating cause: (1) it should not be possible for the factor to exist without interest existing and (2) the factor should not depend on there being interest. Essentialist investigations are not common in economics today but we would argue that it is not because they are without value. Rather, it is because, as Samuelson (1967: 28) confirms, they are out of fashion. Today the essentialist perspective has been largely replaced by a functionalist one. The functionalist seeks to explain economic phenomena of a measurable, or arithmetic, character and does so by constructing mathematical arguments in which their relation to other arithmetic objects is shown. The essentialist, on the other hand, inquires into the origin of the things he wishes to understand. The fundamental difference between the two approaches is in the kind of question they seek to answer.

To give an illustrative example from outside of economics, suppose a functionalist and an essentialist come across a natural pool of water. The functionalist would find something about the pool of water that was measurable – the water level, say – and would seek to relate it to other variables that are present. If he were to find after running a regression that changes in the water level are strongly associated with the number of bathers in the pool, he might propound a number-of-bathers theory of the water level and use his theory for predictive purposes. He might even write down a model showing the exact relationship when specific simplifying assumptions hold. The essentialist, on the other hand, would wonder where the pool of water came from; he would wonder what it was that caused it to exist. The number-of-bathers theory of the water level would not satisfy him because, despite its predictive power, it does not say anything about the originating cause. The essentialist would begin his search for the originating cause by considering various hypotheses, working to assess their logical sense and their *prima facie* empirical plausibility. It is this beginning step that we have taken in this chapter. We have examined various candidates that have been suggested in the literature over the years and have been led to reject three of them: (1) The preference for present over future consumption was rejected on the ground of its *prima facie* empirical implausibility. For this preference to be the originating cause, it would have to be the case that in a given period the amount that consumers would want to borrow for consumption at a zero rate of interest would exceed the amount of saving. A casual empiricism suggests that such an excess demand for consumption loans would not occur. (2) The physical productivity of capital was rejected as the originating cause on logical grounds: the argument is missing an important link and without it it is a *non sequitur*. The important link is that which connects physical productivity with a surplus valued in the unit of account. (3) Finally, value productivity was rejected on the grounds that it arises as a result of interest and originating causes, by our criteria, cannot be the result of the thing that they are supposed to cause.[3]

With two candidates we could find no reason on either *a priori* or *prima facie* grounds for rejecting them. They are liquidity preference, the factor suggested by Keynes in the *General Theory* (1936), and the expectation of entrepreneurial profits, suggested by Schumpeter in his *Theory of Economic Development* ([1911] 1961). While the analysis in this chapter has not yielded a definitive answer to the question of the essence of interest, it constitutes an important, and necessary, first step. A definitive answer would require a complete theory that integrates an explanation of the essence of interest with an explanation of what determines the level of interest actually experienced. The analysis in this chapter serves only to clear the ground on which such a theory can be erected.

Going back to our pool analogy, suppose the essentialist who wants to know how the pool came into being has completed the first step of considering various hypotheses and checking them for *prima facie* empirical plausibility and logical sense. After rejecting several candidates on these grounds, he is left with just two: (1) the pool is caused by an underground spring and (2) the pool is caused by the run-off from melting snows. At this point, he finds that his 'armchair reasoning' can take him no further. He feels compelled to formulate a complete theory showing the full causal chain, starting with the magnitude of the supposed originating cause and relating it to the level of the water in the pool. In addition, he needs to take into account all the other determining factors. The number of bathers in the pool, for example, would need to figure in the theory. Similarly, we need now to develop an empirically based theory that shows *how* a contending originating cause exerts its influence on the interest rate. The essentialist's complete theory is similar to the functionalist's theory in concerning itself with the size of the phenomena in question. In other respects, however, the approaches remain distinct. When an essentialist concerns himself with explaining the level of interest, he does not cease to want to know its originating cause. The functionalist, on the other hand, only wants to construct a model that predicts accurately: originating causes do not interest him.

The analysis in this chapter should guide one in selecting simplifying assumptions when a more complete theory is developed. Our knowledge that liquidity preference or the expected super-productivity of capital could be originating causes of interest warns us against developing a theory that abstracts from either liquid assets or entrepreneurial expectation. Moreover, since the expected super-productivity of capital is a disequilibrium phenomenon, we must be wary of assuming all markets clear immediately. Rather, an analysis that incorporates the insight that some markets adjust more slowly than others is in order.

Much of the aridity of the debate over the originating cause of interest in the early part of this century (see Fetter [1902, 1914] 1977; Seager 1912; Brown 1913, 1914) is due to neglect of these factors by both sides. The school attributing interest to the preference for present over future consumption thought it only necessary to refute the hypothesis that the cause of interest is the productivity of capital; while the productivity school thought it only necessary to refute the hypothesis that it is the preference for present over future consumption. The strength of each side's conviction that it was right was based partly on their conviction that the other side was wrong. They did not consider the possibility that they both might be wrong.

This chapter brings the essentialist discussion up to date by considering a broader range of candidates. Unfortunately, the result offers less certainty than was achieved by the participants in the earlier debate. The analysis, however, serves the purpose of clearing the ground and allows us to see more distinctly the appropriate path to take in developing a more complete theory of interest.

Chapter 4

A causal process analysis of equilibrium in the cash–debt market

In the previous chapter we addressed the question of the originating cause of interest. The resulting discussion served to clear the ground but in itself does not constitute a complete explanation. A reader sceptical about a liquidity preference theory, for instance, might agree with our conclusion that the existence of liquidity preference implies that wealth-holders require some payment to persuade them to give up cash in exchange for debt; but the reader might not be convinced that the payment required to persuade the wealth-holder is as large as the interest rate that we normally observe. All that we have succeeded in demonstrating so far is that the payment must be positive. Further theory is necessary to link liquidity preference to the rate of interest that is observed in the marketplace.

In this chapter, we attempt a more complete causal theory. In order to present it, we specify in greater detail the particular type of economy that we are analysing. In the previous chapter, we discussed the existence of interest within the context of a highly generalized economy. In this chapter, we hope to achieve richer results through incorporating more institutional detail into the theory. Specifically, we want to discuss the determination of interest within an economy with advanced financial markets of the type that characterize the modern day economy.

We begin by sketching out the characteristics of such an economy. Our focus is on the speculative activity of the wealth-holders[1] and the implications of this activity for the determination of price within the bond market. The discussion of speculation leads us to what we call the responsiveness postulate, an empirical postulate that might reasonably characterize an economy with well-developed financial markets in which trading is active. After having sketched broadly the empirical characteristics of the type of economy that we wish to analyse, we construct a simplified model of such an economy. Our aim is to abstract from non-essential detail so that analysis is more manageable.

The subsequent discussion of the model economy takes the form of thought experiments. We introduce, one by one, changes in the various factors that come into play in the bond market. We then examine the causal process that might emanate from each change. Our conclusion is that changes in what have traditionally been deemed the 'real' factors, that is, changes in the willingness to save or changes in capital investment opportunities, need not have any significant direct effect on the interest rate. We find, on the other hand, that changes in wealth-holders' liquidity preferences can have a marked effect.

Other restatements of the liquidity preference theory (see Modigliani 1944: 72; Leijonhufvud 1981: 171) have viewed liquidity preference induced changes in the rate of interest as short-run fluctuations around a long-run, natural rate of interest. The natural rate, in turn, is assumed to play the role of coordinating saving and investment. We depart from these earlier treatments in maintaining that an equilibrium in the real sector is possible without the requirement that a natural rate of interest play a coordinating role.

SPECULATION, LIQUIDITY PREFERENCE AND THE RESPONSIVENESS POSTULATE

On any given trading day, a certain number of bonds are sold to raise money to purchase investment goods and a certain number are bought to serve as a vehicle for new saving. But then there are trades that are unrelated to the current flows of investment and saving. Existing bonds are bought and sold by wealth-holders who are only rearranging their existing portfolios. It is customary to think of the latter type of trading as speculation.[2] The primary motivation behind much of the trading is the expectation of securing a profit from future price changes.

There is little consensus among economists about how speculation should be viewed. On the one hand, there are those who like to quote Keynes' (1936: 159) memorable words on the subject: 'Speculators may do no harm as bubbles on a steady stream of enterprise. But the position is serious when enterprise becomes the bubble on a whirlpool of speculation. When the capital development of the country becomes a by-product of the activities of a casino, the job is likely to be ill-done.' Yet on the other hand, there is the venerable tradition of viewing speculation as essentially stabilizing. The opinion expressed by John Stuart Mill ([1848] 1909: 705) that 'the prices of things are neither so much depressed at one time, nor so much raised at another, as they would be if speculative dealers did not exist' is still widely held.

The two opposing camps have one point in common, however. They both view speculation as a modifying influence on price; they differ only on the question of whether price is modified for ill or good. Implicit in both is a theory of the determination of price in the absence of speculation. Only with such a theory in mind can one analytically separate out the effect of speculation. We will proceed somewhat differently in incorporating speculation into the theory from the start. We wish to present a theory of the determination of interest in an economy with advanced financial markets in which speculation is pervasive. The question of the determination of the interest rate under a different institutional arrangement, in which speculation does not exist, will not be addressed directly.

We can begin by making a distinction between two different types of motive that will compel a speculator to trade in the bond market. First, there is what we could call the general speculative motive that leads a speculator to trade bonds for cash in order to keep investment options open. Cash provides the liquidity necessary to seize any sudden investment opportunity that may come along. The consequence of this motive towards liquidity is not action but inaction; the impulse is to defer decision. It arises when a speculator is unwilling to commit to a particular asset because something better than the existing opportunities might come along. We call it the general speculative motive since it refers to speculation in general and not to speculation about anything in particular. As we argue in Chapter 2, the general speculative motive is one of the reasons contributing to a liquidity preference.

Contrasted with the general speculative motive is the particular speculative motive of Keynes' *General Theory*. Keynes defines it as the 'object of securing profit from knowing better than the market what the future will bring forth' (1936: 170). The type of speculation that Keynes associates with the determination of the rate of interest is speculation about the future price of bonds. While the general speculative motive leads to indecisive inaction during moments when one feels uncertain about the future, Keynes' speculative motive leads to decisive action at points at which one thinks one 'knows better than the market'.

Traditionally, interpreters of Keynes have emphasized the particular speculative motive and have ignored the general. The result has been two criticisms that have been levelled against his liquidity preference theory of interest that otherwise might have been averted. One criticism is that the theory appears to be pulling itself up by its bootstraps. If it is the case that the theory relies on the particular speculative motive to explain interest and the particular speculative motive refers to speculation about the future rate of interest, then it seems that

> the rate of interest is what it is because it is expected to become other than it is; if it is not expected to become other than it is, there is nothing left to tell us why it is what it is. The organ which secretes it has been amputated, and yet it somehow still exists – a grin without a cat.
>
> (Robertson 1940: 25)

We have already given one response to the criticism, which is to say that the expectation of a thing could be a causal precedent of the thing itself. But leaving that argument aside, one can also answer the bootstrap criticism by saying that interest can be explained by reference to the general speculative motive without any reference to speculation about the future rate of interest. The general speculative motive means one demands a positive rate of interest simply to compensate for the loss of another, possibly more profitable, investment opportunity.

The other criticism levelled against a liquidity preference theory that could be averted by making the distinction between a general and a particular speculative motive is the criticism that a liquidity preference theory only makes sense for an economy with advanced bond markets in which speculative trades take place. The question that is raised is what would determine the interest rate in an economy without the institutions necessary for speculative trading in bonds. The answer is that the general speculative motive can operate without the existence of an organized bond market. A wealth-holder with cash to lend can still speculate that some other type of investment opportunity might arise and demand interest to compensate for the loss of such a possibility. It is true that the stage of development of the financial institutions should affect the causal process through which the interest rate is determined. But beyond the institutions is the subjective factor of liquidity preference that might well be universal. Any theory of interest, therefore, needs to take account of it.

In sum, the general speculative motive is associated with the subjective factor of liquidity preference that might well exist in any economy. The particular speculative motive, on the other hand, presupposes a particular market structure characterized by organized bond markets. In this chapter we want to explore the causal process through which the interest rate is determined when the particular speculative motive is operating in full force. The results we achieve in this chapter, therefore, will not apply as generally as the results from the previous chapter but will have the compensating virtue of being more specific.

In an economy in which there are a large number of speculative trades between cash and bonds, there arises the possibility that, in any period, the non-speculative trades arising from saving and investment are overwhelmed to such an extent that they exert little effect. Such a situation could arise when speculators are highly responsive to small changes in the interest rate. Suppose, for instance, that there is a sharp increase in corporate investment causing an influx of new bonds into the loanable funds market. Traditional theory would predict a rise in the interest rate. But if speculators are active, they may see a small change in the interest rate arising from the new bond issues and immediately respond by selling or buying bonds: those who think that the small rise is an indication that bond prices have peaked will sell and those who think that it is an indication that they are on an upward trend will buy. No-one can say *a priori* whether the bulls or the bears will dominate but what one can say is that the resulting level of the interest rate will probably be different from what it would be if the speculators were not involved. We shall refer to this possibility that speculative wealth-holders react to any perceptible change in the interest rate as the responsiveness postulate.

Acceptance of the responsiveness postulate does not

necessarily imply that one thinks that the real factors are irrelevant for the determination of the interest rate. One can allow that speculators dominate in the same way in the stock market but still admit that the profitability of a given company will influence the price of its stock. Speculators in the stock market try to predict future profits and trade accordingly. If a prediction turns out to be wrong, there will be an eventual correction in the price. The real factors exert their influence either through being correctly anticipated by the speculators or later, as mistakes are corrected. In the stock market, therefore, one can reasonably think of speculation as determining short-run price movements but allow that in the long-run, real forces will dominate. Similarly, all we wish to postulate at this stage in the argument is that in the loanable funds market, in any given period, trades by speculative wealth-holders can determine interest rate movements.

There are two versions of the responsiveness postulate that can be identified: the strong and the weak. The strong version says that if a change in real forces causes pressure on the interest rate, speculators will behave in such a way as to defuse that pressure. For example, if an increase in savings coming onto the loanable funds market leads to downward pressure on the interest rate, then speculators will tend to sell bonds and counterbalance the downward effect. The weak version, on the other hand, merely says that wealth-holders react to changes in the interest rate but does not specify in what direction. It is the strong version that is consistent with Keynes' (1936: 201–3) hypothesis that speculators form an idea of a 'safe' rate of interest. According to Keynes, if the actual rate of interest falls relative to this safe rate, as in our example, then speculators will increase their holdings of cash. The opposite will occur if the interest rate rises.

The standard interpretation of Keynes' hypothesis about wealth-holder behaviour is that it implies that one's speculative holdings will consist solely of bonds or solely of money (Tobin 1958: 70; Chick 1983: 204). It can be shown, however, that if one's expectation of the future rate of interest is held with uncertainty, it is reasonable to diversify. Suppose one's uncertain expectation of the 'safe' value of the long-term interest rate is 10 per cent. As the long-term rate edges up towards 10 per cent, one might gradually relinquish more liquid assets in order to lock into long-term bonds. If it was certain that the interest rate would reach 10 per cent, one would maintain a completely liquid portfolio until it hit that point. But because it is uncertain, one proceeds more cautiously and alters the portfolio over a range of changes in the interest rate.

The weak version of the responsiveness postulate does not entail as restrictive an assumption about wealth-holder behaviour. It merely says that wealth-holders are responsive to changes in the interest rate without specifying what they will do in response. The scenario that Keynes paints may come about but it is just as likely that expectations will shift and that one's former estimate of the safe rate of interest will be revised. Shackle's interpretation of Keynes leads to the weak version of the responsiveness postulate. Like Kahn (1954: 250), Shackle is critical of Keynes' attempt to describe a stable functional relationship between the rate of interest and the level of speculative balances demanded and writes that if one insists on drawing such a curve, then 'this curve must be looked upon as a thread floating in a gusty wind, continually liable to change its form' (Shackle 1967: 217).

The responsiveness postulate does not require that each speculator responds every time the interest rate moves. Rather, it only requires that with each small movement, the response of wealth-holders, taken as a group, is significant. For any speculative saver, there may be only a small range of possible values of the interest rate over which he is reactive. Yet if speculators are very different in their views on how to beat the market (as casual observation suggests they are), then as a group, they will be reactive over the entire range. The postulate should not be confused with the hypothesis, commonly associated with the liquidity preference theory, that the demand for money is elastic with respect to the interest rate. Wealth-holders might be highly responsive to changes in the interest rate and one could still find the demand for money inelastic with respect to the interest rate. One reason is that the elasticity gives the ratio of a proportional change in the money demand to a proportional change in the interest rate. The responsiveness postulate, however, says that a small change in the interest rate will bring about a large change, in absolute terms, in speculative cash balances. That is to say, the change will be large enough to overwhelm the change in the demand for cash precipitated by the change in real conditions. Moreover, if wealth-holders are responding in different ways, with one set buying bonds and another set selling, then their activity will not show up in the elasticity measure.

The responsiveness postulate is more relevant under some institutional arrangements than others. In an economy with a small stock of financial wealth or with poorly organized financial markets, for instance, it may not hold true that small changes in interest rates elicit much speculative activity. A small stock of financial wealth would mean that, even if speculation was taking place, the volume of speculative flows might be small relative to the volume of non-speculative activity in the loanable funds market. In this case, it would be more likely that real forces would exert a direct influence on interest rates. If financial markets are poorly organized, it is more costly to effect the transactions necessary to alter the liquidity of a portfolio. The result would be less speculative trading and thus less of the responsiveness that we have postulated. In today's advanced economies, however, the postulate is probably better justified than it has ever been. The leverage afforded professional bond dealers through repurchase agreements and other means allows them to speculate with much more wealth than they actually own.[3] The increasing globalization of financial markets has greatly expanded the relevant stock of financial wealth, meaning that a few speculative transactions in the current stock of debt can easily swamp even a large change in the flow of new issues. Adding to the relevance of the postulate is the trend away from inactive individual portfolios towards aggressively managed mutual funds which has heightened the amount of speculative activity. This trend has the effect of making wealth-holders as a group more reactive at each level of the interest rate.

To sum up, our discussion of speculation in the bond market led us to the distinction between the general speculative motive and the particular speculative motive. The general speculative motive refers to a wealth-holder's inclination towards liquidity as a means of keeping investment options open. We note that it is the general speculative motive that is linked to liquidity preference as we defined it earlier. The particular speculative motive, on the other hand, refers to a wealth-holder's urge to trade deriving from a belief that he knows 'better than the market' the future course of interest rates.

In an economy in which a substantial number of wealth-holders are driven by the particular speculative motive, it is possible that, in the short-run at least, changes in the real factors underlying the loanable funds market will be overwhelmed so that they exert no perceptible effect on the rate of interest. We suggest that such a situation might arise if what we call the responsiveness postulate holds true. We now develop more fully the implication of the responsiveness postulate for the theory of interest. We have argued that in the short-run, the so-called 'real' factors may be overwhelmed; we now need to address the more involved question of the long-run. In order to make the task more manageable, however, it is necessary first to present a simplified model of the cash–debt market.

A SIMPLIFIED CASH–DEBT MARKET

Having defined interest as the premium paid when one purchases a present claim denominated in the unit of account with a future claim, it is reasonable to suppose that the interest rate is determined in the market where these exchanges are made. In this section, we present a simplified version of the market which will serve as the model for our causal process interpretation of the liquidity preference theory.

We begin by supposing a sharp distinction in the minds of asset holders between present unit of account denominated claims – which we shall call cash – and future unit of account denominated claims – which we shall call debt. In the real world the categories are not so clearly defined but roughly, what we call cash corresponds to all those assets that can be transformed into immediate purchasing power without delay or transactions costs. Currency and current account bank deposits would fall into this category. Although in the real world debt is available in a continuum of maturities, we shall suppose, for the sake of simplicity, that only long-term debt is available. We are abstracting from short-term debt (including the kind of debts that are termed cash by investors). This assumption may seem to skirt the objection to the liquidity preference theory that it can only explain the differential between short- and long-term interest rates but that it cannot explain the short-term rate. As we argue in Chapter 2, however, our working hypothesis is that short-term interest rates can be regarded as deriving from long-term rates. This hypothesis does not rule out the possibility that autonomous changes in the short-term rate may react on the long-term rate, it only says that the long term rate is more fundamental.

We divide the cash–debt market into three sets of principal players: (1) consumers who earn factor incomes, buy consumption goods, and incur consumer debt liabilities; (2) producers who buy producer goods and incur producer debt liabilities; and (3) wealth-holders who are in possession of the consumer and producer debt assets corresponding to the other players' liabilities and who hold cash as a store of wealth. This division into three sets of players is only for conceptual purposes and does not rule out the possibility of an economic agent playing more than one role. A consumer, for example, to the extent that he is a saver, will also be a wealth-holder.

Although the government is a major player in the real world cash–debt market, we are abstracting from its actions. The reason is that we wish first to understand how the rate of interest is determined in a 'free market' before bringing in the complicating influence of fiscal policy. The same rationale leads us to abstract from central bank influence on the monetary base. Treating the monetary base as exogenous is standard practice for many economists. Increasingly, however, the decision to do so has come under attack. Moore (1988), for instance, argues that central banks have no choice but to accommodate to loan demand. He allows that the central bank could increase the quantity of high powered money if it desired but that it cannot cause it to contract it if loan demand is high. A central bank's inability to contract the monetary base is, according to Moore (1988: xi), 'a logical necessity arising out of the nature of money and finance in all modern credit money economies'.

The conventional view is that through selling bonds in the open market, the central bank contracts the monetary base. Moore's position is that if loan demand is high and money is tight, banks will satisfy loan demand by borrowing at the discount window. Only through raising the discount rate sufficiently can the central bank cause the amount of bank lending to fall. On the basis of the idea of banks using the discount window as a routine source of funds, Moore concludes the supply curve for money is a horizontal line with its level determined by the discount rate.

Moore's assumption that banks are free to use the discount window routinely is at odds with the overt position of, for instance, the United States Federal Reserve, that borrowing at the discount window is a privilege not a right and intended to be used only in emergencies. If a bank makes frequent use of the window, the Federal Reserve calls the bank to ask what the problem is and how it intends to remedy it. If borrowing persists, the borrowing privilege can be revoked. It would seem that the banks perceive these threats as credible since it is rare that borrowing is not curtailed after an administrative counselling call (Stigum 1983: 254). In addition, the fact that even when the Federal Funds rate is above the discount rate, banks borrow in the Federal Funds market rather than at the discount window, again suggests that they do not regard the discount window as a routine source of funds.

If it were true that the money supply was perfectly elastic at an interest rate set by the central bank, as Moore contends, then there would be no need for a theory of interest. The interest rate is a policy variable. Our position is that even if it were the case that the monetary authorities were pegging the interest rate, it is useful nevertheless to ask what would happen to the interest rate if the monetary authorities were to relinquish control and adopt a more *laissez faire* stance. An analogous case is one in which a physiologist would want to understand the complete course of a condition of gangrene, even if it were argued that in a society with a modern health-care system, a doctor would intervene before the disease progressed very far.

While we disagree with what might be called the extreme endogenous money position that the monetary base be regarded as perfectly elastic at the central bank's discount rate, we agree with a more moderate position that the size of the total money supply will vary with the level of demand for loans. We shall allow, therefore, in our simplified economy, for the existence of a banking system which in addition to acting as an intermediary between the three sets of players mentioned above, has some role in the cash–debt market. We will allow that the money multiplier through which the monetary base is translated into the total stock of money has a certain amount of elasticity. In periods of strong demand for loans, banks will tend to extend more credit from a given deposit base (although the amount of credit that they can extend is not without limit). Various financial instruments can be employed to minimize reserve requirements and they will be employed more vigorously in times of high loan demand.

Moreover, in recessionary periods, especially when uncertainty about borrowers' ability to repay is increased, bankers may restrict credit expansion and allow reserves to accumulate. For completeness, we shall also recognize the existence of a market in which banks lend and borrow each other's reserves. To assume an endogenous money supply and to ignore this market could give an overly distorted result.

One can think of each of the principal players in the cash–debt market possessing, at the beginning of a hypothetical period, a given endowment. Consumers, who are also the factor owners, are endowed with cash income earned in the previous period and a stock of consumer debt liabilities. Producers begin with cash representing retained earnings from the previous period (which can be thought to include a fund of money working capital), a stock of producer debt liabilities and the goods that were produced in the previous period which they intend to sell in this period. Finally, wealth-holders start the period with the stock of consumer and producer debt assets as well as the stock of cash that had been used in the previous period to satisfy their desire to hold some of their wealth in the most liquid asset.

When the period begins, the players begin making exchanges and continue until each is satisfied with his holdings of cash and debt at the reigning interest rate. A consumer will borrow or lend up to the point that the premium he is willing to pay in order to consume now rather than in the future is equal to the interest rate; a producer will issue new debt as long as the interest rate is below the expected profitability of new investment; and a wealth-holder will adjust his portfolio until his desire for liquidity is satisfied at the going rate of interest.

In presenting this simple cash–debt market and identifying the conditions that must hold if it is to be in equilibrium, we are not departing too far from the traditional neoclassical presentations of the theory of interest – the classic statement being Fisher's (1930) volume. Where we depart most radically from those presentations, however, is in our subsequent analysis of the equilibrium. After having identified the equilibrium conditions, Fisher proceeded by writing down a system of simultaneous equations which could be said to 'determine' the interest rate. We take the alternative tack of attempting to describe the causal sequence of events through which equilibrium is attained after it has been disturbed. In adopting this alternative mode of economic explanation, we arrive at a different sort of conclusion from that arrived at by the more traditional general equilibrium approach.

SOME CONCEPTUAL EXPERIMENTS

We have argued already that short-run, day-to-day movements in the interest rate may be the result of speculation. Now we address the question of whether, in the long-run, the so-called real factors exert an influence. A problem with many accounts of the liquidity preference theory that stress the speculative character of the interest rate is that they do not address the question of the role of the non-speculative traders. Those who believe in the influence of productivity and thrift are given no reason to doubt that these factors are operating in the background determining some kind of long-run, or centre of gravity, rate of interest. Our aim in this section is to show more clearly how the non-speculative factors come into play in the cash–debt market. To this end, we shall do a number of conceptual experiments in which we postulate changes in the various factors that operate in the cash–debt market and then analyse the causal processes that emanate from each change.

In order to simplify our exposition of the causal process, we shall assume, in the first instance, that the market participants' inflationary expectations are unaltered by the changes in the real factors that we introduce. The assumption is, admittedly, an unrealistic one. In the real world, the interest rate is influenced considerably by changing expectations of the future rate of inflation, and these expectations are influenced by the type of variations that we are postulating. Our purpose in abstracting from them is to analyse that part of the interest rate that would exist in their absence. After that job is done, we can then relax the assumption and allow for the operation of an inflationary premium.

First, suppose that consumers decide to increase their rate of saving. We can think of each consumer having a schedule of the amount that would be saved out of each level of income, the greater the level of income the higher the proportion of income that would be saved. The hypothesized change could be represented as a shift of the schedule so that at each level of income the consumer saves more. The first period effect of the increase in saving will be an excess demand for debt assets, as savers seek out vehicles for their savings. Normally, one would infer from this situation a fall in the interest rate to clear the market. But our responsiveness postulate, introduced above, says that due to the existence of speculative trading, we cannot be assured that the interest rate will move in line with changes in the so-called real factors – at least, not in the short-run. It would seem, however, that if the demand for debt assets has increased, then eventually the effect would be felt. Even with speculation operating, it would seem that if the demand has increased, interest rates would be lower than they would be if demand had not changed.

One must consider, however, that by the next period the increase in the saving rate will have precipitated a fall in incomes of those who work in the consumer goods industries. In the second period, therefore, the increased demand for debt assets by savers may not get a chance to exert its influence on the interest rate because the increased savings of one group will be met by the decreased savings of another.

The standard objection to this paradox of thrift effect is that when consumer spending goes down, investment spending will go up, leaving aggregate income unchanged. The mechanism through which the balancing of the two components of aggregate demand is achieved, however, is normally thought to be the interest rate. It is required that the increased saving translates automatically into a fall in the interest rate and a rise in investment. Our point of departure from this line of analysis is our position that on a day-to-day basis, the interest rate can be subject to movements determined by speculative trading. The result is that the interest rate cannot be relied on to ensure that investment spending will move in a direction opposite to consumer spending. If investment and consumption do not move in opposite directions, then the paradox of thrift comes into play.

At a lower level of income, the transactions demand for money will be reduced and one might argue that the interest rate will be reduced through this route. The effect is limited, however, by the endogenity of the money supply that we describe in the section above. As the economy slows, banks may extend less credit from a given deposit base. When the demand for loans is weak and reserves are ample, fewer techniques will be employed to skirt reserve requirements and some banks may allow reserves to accumulate.

It is inaccurate to assume, however, that the money supply adapts perfectly to a change in demand. Rather than keeping reserves idle, banks will often attempt to lend them out to other banks on an overnight basis, on what is known in the United States as the Federal Funds market. To the extent that they do so, the reduced demand for money to meet the needs of trade will lead to a reduction in the Federal Funds rate of interest. If the longer term rate of interest is to be affected, then, by the increase in the desire to save, it has to be through a reduction in the Federal Funds rate working its way through the term structure. A link can be found, therefore, but it is a weak and indirect one.

The causal process associated with a reduction in the desire to save parallels the one we describe above for an increase. The demand for debt assets by savers will fall but given the magnitude of speculative trading in existing assets that occurs in a modern financial system, the effect on the interest rate of a reduction in demand by savers can easily be obscured. If the money supply has some elasticity in response to a change in demand, money incomes will rise. The increase will be due to a rise in prices, a rise in output, or both, depending on the amount of slack in the economy. The result is that, by the next period, even if all consumers are saving a smaller proportion of their money income, the total quantity of saving will not necessarily be lower. An increase in the interest rate, therefore, is not directly caused by an increase in saving. Again, if the effect is to be felt, it will be through the increased demand for cash to finance a higher level of activity. The strength of this effect again will depend on how much credit can be expanded relative to the increase in economic activity.

Both an increase and a decrease in the rate of saving will lead to a disequilibrium in the consumer goods industry which will likely reverberate into the markets for factors of production. We will not venture to answer the question of how a general equilibrium, in which all markets clear simultaneously, might be reestablished. Our position is that in individual markets, prices adjust in response to excess demands or supplies, but that there is no obvious mechanism to ensure that all markets equilibrate simultaneously. Our focus here is on the cash–debt market, and equilibrating tendencies in other markets are brought in only if they appear to have a palpable effect on the market under scrutiny.

Now consider the effect on the interest rate of an increase in the expected profitability of new investment. The demand for debt liabilities increases but in the short-run the effect on the interest rate is likely to be washed out by the speculative trading that is a fact of modern financial systems. Money incomes increase as new investment is carried out and by the next period savings have increased to match the level of investment. Again, if there is pressure on the interest rate, it will not be through the saving–investment relation but through a shortage of cash to finance the growth in money incomes. The shortage will show up, if at all, in the Federal Funds market. The long term rate of interest will be affected only if the rise in the Federal Funds rate was to spread through the term structure.

As long as the expected profitability of new investment remains above the interest rate, the cash–debt market will be out of equilibrium. Traditional theory says that the interest rate will adjust to the expected profitability. One cannot rule out the possibility, however, that it will be the expected profitability that will adjust to the interest rate. As new investment is carried out, two things can happen that will reduce the profitability of any further investment. First, the prices of the inputs of the production process can rise as producers compete for them, and second, the prices of the output can fall as expanded capacity causes more output to be available. Either event will cause a divergence between the value of the output and the value of the input to shrink, reducing the expected profitability of any further investment.

The case of a decline in the expected profitability of investment is analogous. No imbalance of saving and investment need result; if the interest rate is influenced at all, it will be through a decline in the amount of cash required to finance a lower rate of economic activity. In the event that the interest rate is left unaffected, a new equilibrium can be restored through the expected profitability of investment rebounding due to a fall in price of unemployed inputs, or an increase in the price of output as the reduction in investment causes it to become more scarce.

Another factor that weakens further the link between a change in the real factors that we have considered and a change in the interest rate is the operation of Keynes' speculative motive. As we argue above, Keynes hypothesized that if the rate of interest starts to fall relative to what is considered a safe rate, then wealth-holders will sell bonds and demand cash. By doing so the wealth-holders produce a countervailing force against the fall in the interest rate. The objection to Keynes' speculative motive, however, is that his assumption about wealth-holder behaviour is *ad hoc*. There is no reason to believe that wealth-holders always respond to a fall in the interest rate by selling bonds. They could just as easily interpret a fall in the interest rate as evidence that their estimation of the safe or normal rate was too high and cause them to revise it downward. Nevertheless, the operation of Keynes' speculative motive is a possibility that ought to be considered before drawing any firm connection between the change in the so-called real factors and the rate of interest.

Up to this point we have been abstracting from the premium that market participants factor into the interest rate to compensate for the possible erosion of purchasing power of the principal of the debt. This premium is arguably the most volatile component of real world interest rates and the factor to pay attention to if one wants to predict their future course. We have abstracted from it up to this point in order that the other, less powerful, forces could be analysed. But if a change in saving or investment is of sufficient magnitude to cause pressure on the interest rate due to a shortage of cash, the inflationary premium will often be affected as well. If economic activity increases due to a fall in saving or an increase in investment, the effect might show up in price levels and inflationary expectations will produce a higher rate of interest. The higher rate will tend to cause certain types of spending to be curtailed. For instance, if the rise is considered temporary and if it is believed to overcompensate for future inflation, it might cause a postponement in durable goods and housing purchases until the interest rate went back to what are thought to be more normal levels. In this case, the interest rate operates to cool the economy, just as it does in traditional theories. Yet the reason behind the mechanism is very different. In a recessionary environment, brought on by less consumer or investment spending, inflationary premia might drop, causing the interest rate to drop and stimulating spending in housing and consumer durables. Again, the interest rate is seen to be operating as an equilibrating force, pulling the economy out of a slump. There is no reason to believe, however, that the mechanism will operate to establish a full employment – it merely operates in the right direction.

Summing up so far, we have examined the effect in the cash–debt market of changes in the desire to save and in changes in the profitability of new investment. We find that if the long-term rate of interest is to be affected, it will be either through a change in the supply and demand conditions for bank reserves or through a change in the inflationary premium component. The strength of the bank reserve effect, however, is questionable and will be limited both by the possible operation of Keynes' speculative motive and by the endogenity of the money supply.

Our final conceptual experiment involves a change in the set of expectations influencing wealth-holders' desire for liquidity. While it is true that wealth-holders are diverse in their expectations, a trend will often emerge out of the diversity. We witness such a trend whenever we see stock prices moving up or down. For a stock to be traded, there must be someone who believes it is a good time to sell while someone else believes it is a good time to buy. Yet despite the obvious and necessary diversity, we can often characterize the aggregate market sentiment as bullish or bearish. Take, for example, an event like the invasion of Kuwait in 1990 which had the effect of increasing the amount of uncertainty about future economic conditions. Such an event can produce a direct effect on liquidity preference inducing wealth-holders to go into cash; or, to put it differently, causing them to insist on a higher reward for going out of cash. If, at the initial interest rate, wealth-holders on average want to increase their holdings of cash, from, say, 5 per cent to 10 per cent of their total portfolios, the effect on the interest rate could be pronounced. Unlike in the case of an increase in the demand for cash for consumer or, especially, investment spending, wealth-holders normally will not increase their cash holdings by borrowing. The implication is that the elasticity of supply of money cannot be relied on to satisfy demand. The only ways a wealth-holder can increase his cash holding is either by convincing another wealth-holder to decrease his holding or by convincing a consumer or producer to give up cash holdings that would have gone to finance a real transaction and use it to buy a debt asset instead.

If the increased uncertainty involves a reduction in confidence that the interest will not rise, then one wealth-holder can convince another to give up cash only by selling him debt at a much reduced price. Consumers and producers might be responsive in their marginal spending to smaller changes in the interest rate, yet because the size of interest-sensitive spending is so small relative to even 5 per cent of the total stock of wealth, it would similarly require a large change in the interest rate to drum up cash from these sources.

In an analogous way, a reduction in liquidity preference could easily bring about a marked decline in the interest rate. Wealth-holders, less worried that bond prices will unexpectedly tumble, will try to increase their holdings of debt, causing its price to increase. Consumers and producers are able to issue debt on more favourable terms and will do so; but, as a proportion of total debt assets, the magnitude of the increase in the flow is likely to be small. The restoration of equilibrium is more readily restored through the effect of a falling interest rate in allaying the desire for debt.

The conditions necessary for equilibrium in the cash–debt market are that the rate of interest be equal to the marginal rate of time preference, the marginal expected profitability of capital, and the 'marginal rate of liquidity preference', where the last is defined as the reward one must pay the marginal wealth-holders to convince them to hold a future claim denominated in the unit of account. In our three conceptual experiments, we supposed that each of these marginal conditions was violated and then examined the market processes through which equilibrium would be restored.

We found in the case of a change in the marginal rate of time preference or the marginal profitability of capital, that market forces lead to no necessary change in the interest rate. Rather, the brunt of the adjustment can be in changes in the relative prices and the quantities of consumer and producer goods, that is, in the markets that are directly affected by the change. In the case of a change in the marginal rate of liquidity preference, however, the adjustment process showed just the opposite. Some modification in the marginal rate of liquidity preference could be expected as cash is either released from or absorbed by consumers and producers. Yet since this flow is small relative to the portfolio alteration that a change in liquidity preference can easily entail, movement in the interest rate is necessary for the greater part of the adjustment. Our conceptual experiments indicate, therefore, that in the absence of inflationary expectations, anything more than a slight, temporary, change in the interest rate is more likely to be due to a change in liquidity preference than to a change in the demand for credit from consumers or producers. To borrow a Keynesian phrase, the marginal rate of liquidity preference can be thought to 'rule the roost': that is to say, it is the marginal rate of liquidity preference, rather than the marginal rate of time preference or the marginal efficiency of capital, that can dominate in setting the level of the interest rate at which equilibrium in the cash–debt market will be established.

THE ROLE OF SAVING AND ACCUMULATION

In standard neoclassical theories of interest, saving and accumulation are at the centre of the explanation. Consider, for example, a Solow-type growth model in which one assumes (1) a single good used both as capital and as a consumption good; (2) continuous full employment of labour and capital; and (3) a production function that is concave in labour and capital. In this type of model, the interest rate is the marginal product of capital and its connection with the rate of saving and accumulation is clear. Since whatever is not consumed is used in production as capital, the higher the rate of saving, the more capital in the production process, the lower the marginal product of capital, and the lower the interest rate. Similarly, higher levels of accumulation, again represented by higher levels of capital in production, are also associated with a lower rate of interest. While most economists would agree that such a model entails highly artificial assumptions, its implication, *viz.* the association between high levels of saving and accumulation and lower rates of interest, is often affirmed. Yet if it is not on the basis of this type of one-sector, full-employment model, it is not clear how the association is derived.

In the previous section, our conceptual experiments revealed how the interest rate reacts to changes in saving and the rate of accumulation, and we saw that these changes would not necessarily result in any permanent, or long-run, change in the interest rate. In this section, we ask the related question of whether the level of saving or accumulation makes any difference, as the Solow model suggests. The procedure that we shall adopt is to postulate two economies basically identical except for (1) in the level of saving, and (2) in the level of accumulation of capital.

Begin with the role of saving. We must first make explicit the distinction between the aggregate quantity of savings and the propensity to save, and decide which of the two will be the basis of the discussion. Are we asking about the effect on the interest rate of the aggregate quantity of saving or about the effect of the propensity to save? Since our goal is to find the causal roots of economic phenomena in individual decision-making, it would seem to make more sense to focus on the propensity to save. The aggregate quantity of saving is regarded in our scheme as the outcome of decisions to save, so in order to get to the ultimate root of the problem, it is best to start with the factor affecting the decision to save, that is, the propensity or willingness to save.

Consider two closed economies: A in which people are willing to save, say, 20 per cent of their income; and B in which they are willing to save only 5 per cent. Abstracting from government spending and assuming that labour and resources are fully employed, it will be the case that in A, expenditure on investment goods will be higher than in B. So far, there is no discrepancy with the Solow model. A difference emerges only when we consider the implication of the higher level of expenditure on investment goods. Since, in the Solow model, there are neither prices nor money, the interest rate is identified with the marginal physical product of capital. If higher levels of capital are associated with a lower marginal physical product, then the implication for the interest rate of a greater willingness to save is clear. In a more realistic analysis, however, the interest rate is equal in equilibrium to the rate of return, or marginal value product, of capital. If the interest rate is 6 per cent per annum, then $1000 worth of new equipment should yield at least 6 per cent per annum in addition to an amount equal to its depreciation. The marginal value productivity in A will be less than that in B if prices are equivalent in the two economies. Yet we have no reason to believe that to be true. If A is producing more output because of its higher level of capital accumulation, then we would expect that output to be cheaper in terms of labour and raw materials than in B. Yet if the output is worth less in terms of labour and raw materials, the stream of profits from given capital goods will be less, and hence it will be valued lower. One is unable to draw a conclusion about which economy has the higher marginal value productivity of capital. The crucial difference between a one-good economy and multi-good economy with money is that in the latter the interest rate is equal in equilibrium with a ratio of values, while in the former everything can be expressed in physical terms.

The same problem arises when we consider the role of the level of accumulation in the determination of the interest rate. Again consider two economies, A and B, identical in all endowments except that A has twice the capital accumulation of B. For every computer or blast furnace in B, A has two. It will be true that A will be able to produce more output from the same labour and raw materials than will B. It will also be true that the physical marginal product of a capital good in A will be lower: because A is already well-stocked with capital goods, one more computer installed in a typical office in A will be less useful than one more installed in B. However, as in the previous case, it is not clear that this lower physical marginal productivity will translate into a lower marginal value productivity.

CONCLUSION

In this and the previous chapter we have presented a two-pronged account of the liquidity preference theory of interest. The first prong, developed in Chapter 3, is the argument that liquidity preference, as we define it, constitutes a reason for the existence of interest. We maintain that just as much as the factors of productivity and time preference, it needs to be considered as a 'real' factor, and not just a transitory short-run influence. The second prong, which is found in the present chapter, is an attempt to analyse the forces determining the level of the interest rate. We proceed first by constructing a model cash–debt market. We then perform a series of conceptual experiments in which we introduce and analyse the effects of changes in the desire to save, capital investment opportunities, and liquidity preferences. Our findings cast doubt on the usual presumption that time preference and capital productivity are the underlying real factors determining the rate of interest. We show that given the existence of heavy speculative trading, there is only a weak connection between a change in the supposed real factors and the rate of interest, if one disregards any inflationary premium. The connection that exists is through a change in the demand for cash resulting from a change in the level of economic activity. The strength of the connection may be considerably weakened, however, if the supply of money responds endogenously to the demand.

The key difference between our liquidity preference theory and more traditional theories of interest is our focus on speculation, broadly defined as trading in existing assets by wealthholders acting under the influence of uncertain expectations of the future. Interest rate theorists often abstract from speculation and consequently reach very different conclusions. The decision to abstract from speculation is not arbitrary; a number of justifications for the practice can be adduced. One argument is that while speculation may cause fluctuations in a price, it cannot explain the price itself. Here the distinction is being made between explaining the existence of a variable and explaining its level, a distinction that we make ourselves in our two-pronged presentation of the liquidity preference theory. We make the distinction between two types of speculation. One arises from what we call the general speculative motive, which leads one to trade debt for cash in order to increase one's range of options. One does not have in mind any alternative investment in particular, but simply judges that increasing the range of options is relatively more desirable. The general speculative motive is one of the reasons behind liquidity preference, a preference which we argue can be viewed as a 'real' factor, comparable in its effect on the interest rate to the forces of productivity and thrift. The other type of speculation arises from the particular speculative motive. This is the motive that a critic has in mind when saying that speculation cannot explain the existence of interest since it refers only to the expectation that the interest rate will change and that one can profit from the change through the appropriate trading strategy. We allow that it is permissible to abstract from the particular speculative motive if one's goal is only to explain the existence of interest. It is not permissible, however, even if one is only explaining existence, to abstract from the general speculative motive.

A related justification for abstracting from speculation in the theory of interest is the argument that speculation produces only bubbles that eventually will burst. Consider, for example, the effect of speculation on property values. Real estate investors often buy properties only because they believe they can profit from an appreciation. Using our terminology, they are acting under the influence of the particular speculative motive. If enough investors believe the same, property values may rise above the amount that people who plan eventually to use the land are willing to pay. Once the land gets into their hands the speculative bubble bursts. Only as long as one speculative property owner sells to another can the bubble remain intact. It is unreasonable, though, to think that such a situation could continue indefinitely. Eventually, the non-speculative factors will come to the fore. The justification for abstracting from speculation in the theory of property values, then, is that one can see more clearly the influence of the 'real' factors that determine price when the speculative bubbles have been eliminated.

One of the differences, however, between the real estate market and the bond market is that it is not as clear, even *ex post*, when a speculative bubble exists. If liquidity preference is the underlying factor that gives rise to interest in the absence of a speculative bubble, then one has no way of computing what the interest rate is supposed to be. Moreover, since a large proportion of the participants in the bond markets are speculative traders, it is not as unreasonable as in the case of the real estate market to think of bubbles persisting, or of one bubble being replaced soon after by another.

Still another reason for abstracting from speculation is the objection that the existence of speculation implies that the economy is in disequilibrium. The implication is that if one allows for continuous speculation, one is unable to do the kind of equilibrium theorizing that is standard fare for economists. It leaves one in a position of analytical nihilism (Coddington 1983: 60). The answer to this objection lies in our method, which breaks from the convention of deriving results from the conditions of a general economic equilibrium and instead involves a looser form of analysis in which we view some markets equilibrating to a greater degree than others. We allow that bond markets can be in an almost constant state of flux with speculators responding to one bit of news after another. And yet, at the same time, other parts of the economy can be equilibrating. If consumers step up demand, more goods come on board to satisfy demand. If the labour market is tight, wages will rise and induce the work force to provide more labour. The fact that financial markets are in flux does not imply chaos for the rest of the economy. One is able, therefore, to draw theoretical conclusions about equilibrating tendencies in other markets.

Chapter 5

Keynes and the liquidity preference theory of interest

> Those individuals who are endowed with a special genius for the subject and have a powerful economic intuition will often be more right in their conclusions and implicit presumptions than in their explanations and explicit statements.
>
> (John Maynard Keynes, 1924, quoted in Chick 1983: vii)

In understanding a scientific theory, it is often useful to distinguish the context of discovery from the context of justification (Holton 1973: 17). Within the context of discovery, a theorist arrives at conclusions by an intuitive process that may be impossible to reconstruct. The context of justification comes into play when the theorist attempts to communicate his conclusions to the world by writing down a systematic, logically coherent theory. In the present chapter, we examine Keynes' liquidity preference theory of interest keeping this distinction in mind. We argue that while Keynes arrived at what we believe is a correct conclusion – namely, that liquidity preference determines the rate of interest, his exposition of the liquidity preference theory of interest is seriously flawed. At the same time, however, we attempt to show, through drawing on his papers and correspondence surrounding the publication of the *General Theory*, that there is more to his intuitive understanding of the problem of interest than is captured in his formal models.

A full appreciation of Keynes' theory of interest is probably crucial in deciphering his paradoxical unemployment equilibrium result, and in understanding the exact point of his departure from the Classics. In a radio broadcast written at the time he was developing the ideas in his *General Theory*, he says:

There is, I am convinced, a fatal flaw in that part of orthodox reasoning which deals with the theory of what determines the level of effective demand and the volume of employment; the flaw being largely due to *the failure of the classical doctrine to develop a satisfactory theory of the rate of interest.*
                (Keynes [1934] 1973, 13: 489, emphasis added)

And, then in a post-*General Theory* article:

The orthodox theory assumes that we have a knowledge of the future of a kind quite different from that which we actually possess . . . . The hypothesis of a calculable future leads to a wrong interpretation of the principles of behaviour which the need for action compels us to adopt, and to an underestimation of the concealed factors of utter doubt, precariousness, hope and fear. *The result has been a mistaken theory of interest.*
                (Keynes [1937] 1973, 14: 122, emphasis added)

Given the importance that the liquidity preference theory of interest appears to play in his broader scheme, it is unfortunate that Keynes was unable to give a convincing account of it. He was unhappy with his exposition of the liquidity preference theory and had hoped to revise it. In a letter of January 1938, he writes: 'I should like sometime or other to write out more fully my views on liquidity preference and the other matters you discuss, for I agree that the discussion of them in my *General Theory* is far from complete' (Keynes [1938] 1979: 263).

Unfortunately, a combination of heart trouble, his war-time activities and, finally, his death in 1946, conspired against the intended revision and we are left to speculate what it was he had wanted to say.

THE GENESIS OF THE IDEA

Keynes does not pretend to present a novel theory of interest in his *Treatise on Money* (1930). No particular theory is developed or defended there; although he does make use of the Wicksellian distinction between the market rate of interest that is determined in the market for money loans and the natural rate that serves to equilibrate the supply of savings and the demand for investment. Despite Keynes' lack of concern with interest rate theory in the *Treatise*, Shackle (1974: 54) argues that the liquidity preference theory 'is presented in fullest freshness and liveliest colours, and almost in its completed form, in the *Treatise*. It does not emerge there all in one place and in one piece, but seems to take shape under our eyes in Keynes' thought.'

The passages to which Shackle refers are the ones in which Keynes describes the bearish sentiments of wealth-holders and the way in which these sentiments can determine the prices of securities. Keynes himself admits that the concept of liquidity preference has its roots in what he calls bearishness in the *Treatise* but notes an important difference:

> [Bearishness is] there defined as the functional relationship, not between the rate of interest (or price of debts) and the quantity of money, but between the price of assets and debts, taken together, and the quantity of money. This treatment, however, involved a confusion between results due to a change in the rate of interest and those due to a change in the schedule of the marginal efficiency of capital . . . .
>
> (Keynes, 1936: 173–4)

Keynes' ideas about bearishness influencing the price of bonds, and hence the rate of interest, were not at all controversial at the time. There seemed to be general agreement that the prices actually appearing on the market could be affected by such forces, but with the proviso that these forces had only a short-run, transitory effect and that in the long-run, prices were determined by the real forces of productivity and thrift. In the long-run, that is, the market rate of interest comes into conformity, usually through a Wicksellian cumulative process, with a natural rate of interest.

Sometime between the *Treatise* and the *General Theory*, however, Keynes made an important break-through that was to render his subsequent analysis of the rate of interest less palatable. The break-through was his rejection of the idea that the rate of interest is the price that equilibrates the supply of savings and the demand for investment. While Keynes seemed to accept the idea of a natural rate when he wrote the *Treatise*, it is possible that he never thought it through clearly. Evidence is that when he later came to criticize the orthodox theory of interest, he claimed he was unable to find or to recreate for himself any coherent account of it (Keynes [1936] 1979: 223).

Initially, the argument that Keynes presented against the

supply-of-saving-demand-for-investment theory of interest is that savings and investment are identically equal and, therefore, it makes no sense to speak of a price bringing them into equilibrium. The equality of savings and investment follows directly from the way the books are kept. In a given accounting period we can think of the money earned by the sale of consumption goods going back to buy those same consumption goods. That means that whatever is left over, that is, the proceeds from investment, must be equal to the quantity of savings.[1]

This argument, presented in an early draft of the *General Theory* (Keynes, 1973, 14: 475–6), was not easily understood. In discussion over the galleys, Roy Harrod tried to dissuade Keynes from criticizing the orthodox theory on the grounds that saving and investment are identically equal. Harrod argued that the quantity of German lessons supplied in London are identically equal with the quantity demanded and yet we can meaningfully use supply and demand analysis to explain their price. The fact that saving and investment are identically equal, therefore, is not sufficient argument against the supply-of-saving-demand-for-investment theory. Harrod also remarked:

> In order to give you pause for thought, I should like to add that this was the most criticised part of your address in Oxford [February 1935], in which you brought out this argument. Frankly, it convinced no one.
>
> (Harrod [1935] in Keynes 1973, 13: 531)

Keynes' critics seem to have believed that he was making the naïve error of confusing the *ex ante* or hypothetical quantity of saving or investment desired at a given rate of interest, with the *ex post* or actual quantity that might occur at a given rate of interest. While actual saving must necessarily equal actual investment, there is no reason that desired saving need equal desired investment. The implication is that there is no logical error in ascribing to the interest rate the role of bringing desired saving into equality with desired investment.

Keynes may have been wrong to accuse the Classical economists of logical error but his argument against the supply-of-saving-demand-for-investment theory entails more than simply the error of not properly distinguishing between actual and desired quantities. His real reasons for rejecting the idea of the interest rate equilibrating desired investment and saving were probably in part empirical and not purely logical. If, for example, there is an outward shift in the demand for investment curve so that desired investment exceeds desired saving, the Classical theory would predict a rise in the interest rate having the dual effect of dampening investment demand and persuading consumers to save more. The interest rate would continue to rise until desired investment equalled desired saving. Now, from Keynes' point of view, the Classical equilibrating process represented a highly improbable chain of events. First, Keynes (1936: 93) believed that saving was not interest sensitive and second, he believed that small changes in the interest rate could easily induce wealth-holders to change their levels of cash holdings. The equilibrating process that Keynes might have envisioned, therefore, would be a small rise in the interest rate persuading wealth-holders to substitute bonds for cash, satisfying the increased demand for investment funds that way. Once the investment funds have been borrowed, actual investment equals desired investment and, at the same time, it is very possible that actual saving equals desired saving. The implication is that desired investment equals desired saving, but not through the mechanism that the Classical economists envisaged. For Keynes, the true explanation as to why desired investment equals desired saving is that by separate processes, desired investment is brought into equality with actual investment and desired saving is brought into equality with actual saving, and that by an accounting identity actual investment equals actual saving. As Shackle (1967: 239) writes, 'all [Keynes] needed to do was to admit that (*ex ante*) saving and investment *are not brought into equality by anything whatever*, save the purest accident. For they do not confront each other simultaneously in one and the same market.'

Harrod had suggested to Keynes that a better line of attack would be to say that the orthodox theory is flawed because it assumes that the level of income is constant. If the assumption is relaxed, then a shift in the demand for investment curve will bring about a change in income which will in turn cause a shift in the supply of savings. Under these conditions, supply and demand analysis breaks down. To illustrate the argument, Harrod provided Keynes with the one diagram that appears in the *General Theory* (1936: 180). Although Keynes (1973, 13: 551) never accepted Harrod's criticism based on the German lesson analogy, he modified his attack on the orthodox theory when he came to revise the *General Theory* and eliminated a long passage in which he attempted to show that the 'amount of saving . . . is the same thing as the amount of investment, looked at from a different standpoint' (Keynes 1973, 14: 475). Instead, he adopted Harrod's suggested strategy of focussing on the assumption of a constant level of income in the orthodox theory. In doing so, he both misrepresented his own reason for rejecting the orthodox theory and possibly weakened the force of his attack. In saying that the orthodox theory needs to assume a constant level of income, he did not threaten economists who chose to assume continuous market clearing. A variable level of income could be seen to be only a special case in which there was some kind of rigidity causing an obstacle to full employment. It would appear, then, that if there were no such obstacles, the supply-of-saving-demand-for-investment theory would be immune from Keynes' criticism.

Having rejected the idea that the interest rate could be determined by the demand for investment and the supply of savings, Keynes searched for an alternative:

> One naturally began by supposing that the rate of interest must be determined in some sense by productivity – that it was, perhaps, simply the monetary equivalent of the marginal efficiency of capital, the latter being independently fixed by physical and technical considerations in conjunction with the expected demand.
>
> (Keynes [1937] 1973, 14: 212)

In pursuing this tack, Keynes came to discover what had been previously argued by Böhm-Bawerk ([1914] 1959: 2), and more consistently by Fetter ([1902] 1977). His conclusion was that 'this line of approach led repeatedly to what seemed to be circular reasoning'. Keynes realized that the return on capital will depend on the level of profit that can be achieved from using a particular capital good relative to its price. Its price, however, will be determined by the present value of its expected stream of profits and to determine the present value one needs an interest rate. The circle is broken only if one can show that the interest rate is determined independently of the productivity of capital.[2] It was upon realizing this that Keynes:

hit on what I now think to be the true explanation. The resulting theory, whether right or wrong, is exceedingly simple – namely that the rate of interest on a loan of given quality and maturity has to be established at the level which, in the opinion of those who have the opportunity of choice – i.e. of wealth-holders – equalises the attractions of holding idle cash and of holding the loan.

(Keynes [1937] 1973, 14: 212–13)

The verb 'hit on' used to describe his process of discovery suggests almost a moment of inspiration. In another account, he writes: 'Then . . . came the notion of interest as being the meaning of liquidity preference, which became quite clear in my mind the moment I thought of it' (Keynes [1936] 1973: 85).

One might be sceptical of a resolution to the difficult question of the explanation of the rate of interest that comes in a single flash of inspiration. But Keynes' reports of his discovery fit well with Kuhn's description of a scientific breakthrough:

normal science ultimately leads only to the recognition of anomalies and to crises. And these are terminated, not by deliberation and interpretation, but by a relatively sudden and unstructured event like the gestalt switch. Scientists then often speak of the 'scales falling from the eyes' or of the 'lightning flash' that 'inundates' a previously obscure puzzle, enabling its components to be seen in a new way that for the first time permits its solution.

(Kuhn 1970: 122)

Moreover, as Shackle (1974) has argued, the groundwork of the liquidity preference theory had already been thought out by Keynes in his *Treatise on Money*. In the *Treatise*, Keynes had analysed in detail the working of financial markets and was well acquainted with the fact that the bearish sentiment on the part of wealth-holders could determine the price of bonds. All he needed to do was to see that this analysis could serve not just as an explanation of the level of interest in the short-run, but that it might be the long-run explanation as well. It was only when he began to think about interest rate theory seriously that he realized the conventional explanations were flawed and that an alternative long-run theory was needed.

Arriving at the central idea seemed to be quite effortless for

Keynes. The real work began when he attempted to write down a theory that would persuade others. The first task was to communicate exactly what he meant by liquidity and liquidity preference.

THE MEANING OF LIQUIDITY AND LIQUIDITY PREFERENCE IN KEYNES' THEORY

Understanding Keynes' liquidity preference theory of interest is made difficult by the imprecise and often conflicting senses in which he uses the terms liquidity and liquidity preference. In the standard textbook presentations of his theory, liquidity is defined as a quantity of either real or nominal money balances and liquidity preference is then construed as the demand for those balances. Now, while the textbook interpretation can easily be found in Keynes' writings (1936: 202; [1937] 1973, 14: 223), it raises a number of questions. The first is why he framed the curious term 'liquidity preference' instead of more simply calling it the demand for money. The adoption of a different term suggests that he might have had something else in mind. The second question is why, if his theory was simply a supply and demand for money theory, he was so adamant (Keynes [1937] 1973, 14: 202) that it was distinct from and very much at odds with the loanable funds theories being propounded by other theorists at the time (Robertson 1936; Ohlin 1937a, b; Hawtrey 1937: a, b). Those theorists, and others since (Fellner and Somers 1941; Tsiang 1956), have contended that a supply and demand theory for money is equivalent to a supply and demand theory for loanable funds. Keynes' insistence that there was something irreconcilable about his theory and the loanable funds theories could be explained if it was true that by a liquidity preference theory he meant something different from simply saying that the interest rate is determined by the demand for nominal, or real, money balances in relation to the supply.

Recall that in Chapter 2, we defined liquidity as a subjectively determined attribute of an asset reflecting one's estimation of the transactions costs involved in selling it and the degree of certainty one has about the price that would be obtainable. Liquidity preference, we maintained, was the preference for more over less liquidity in one's assets. Under our definition, liquidity preference can give rise to a demand for money but it is not synonymous with it. In Keynes, however, the distinction between the subjective motivation and the market phenomenon to which it gives rise, is blurred. At times liquidity preference appears to be a subjective motivation, for example, when he writes of the 'liquidity preference for money as a means of holding wealth' (Keynes 1936: 168). Yet at other times it can be construed as simply the demand for money (Keynes [1937] 1973, 14: 223).

As we have already noted, Keynes admits that the concept of liquidity preference has roots in the concept of bearishness that was introduced in his Treatise on Money. While the explicit definition that he gives there amounts to a demand function for money, his choice of terms is suggestive. Bearishness suggests a motivation to which only wealth-holders are prone. A wage earner living from pay cheque to pay cheque who holds money for the purposes of making transactions can be said to demand money but it would be an odd use of language to call him 'bearish'. So, even though Keynes was setting out a definition of a demand curve for money, his choice of terms suggests that what he had in mind was a demand for money on the part of wealth-holders only.

In the *General Theory* the tension between a liquidity preference that means the total demand for money and a liquidity preference that is associated with the demand for money by wealth-holders only, persists (Haberler [1939] 1958: 210). Keynes first introduces the term liquidity preference in Chapter 13 of *The General Theory of Interest*. He says there (Keynes 1936: 166) that the 'psychological time-preferences of an individual require two distinct sets of decisions to carry them out completely'. He distinguishes the decision to save from the decision about 'in *what* form he will hold the command over future consumption which he has reserved'. It is in discussing the latter decision that Keynes introduces the idea of a liquidity preference. His conclusion, arrived at on the next page, is as follows:

> Thus the rate of interest at any time, being the reward for parting with liquidity, is a measure of the unwillingness of those who possess money to part with their liquid control over it. The rate of interest is not the 'price' which brings into equilibrium the demand for resources to invest with the readiness to abstain from present consumption. It is the 'price'

which equilibrates the desire to hold wealth in the form of cash with the available quantity of cash.

(Keynes 1936: 167)

From his discussion in Chapter 13, then, we are led to believe that when Keynes wrote of liquidity preference, he was referring to a demand for money on the part of wealth-holders, as distinct from the demand for money on the part of consumers and producers. This interpretation is also suggested by his own summary of the theory in a post-*General Theory* article that we have already quoted. He writes:

[The] theory, whether right or wrong, is exceedingly simple – namely that the rate of interest on a loan of given quality and maturity has to be established at the level which, *in the opinion of those who have the opportunity of choice – i.e. of wealth-holders – equalises the attractions of holding idle cash and of holding the loan.*

(Keynes [1937] 1973, 14: 212–13, emphasis added)

Further on in the *General Theory*, however, the liquidity preference theory of interest is represented by an equilibrium condition in which the total demand for money is equated with the supply (Keynes 1936: 199). This representation, which is the one captured in most formal Keynesian models, obscures the insight that he presents in the earlier chapter: that it is the role of the wealth-holder that is crucial in the determination of the interest rate. In a letter to D.H. Robertson, Keynes admits that at one point in the writing of the *General Theory*, he did change his mind about how he would define liquidity preference:

In my terminology *liquidity preference* relates to the *total* demand for money for all purposes and not merely to the demand for inactive balances. Quite often one needs to distinguish the demand for active balances from the demand for inactive balances. At one time, indeed, I did try to use separate terms and drafted for about a year on these lines. But I found that in making general statements this involved an enormous amount of verbiage; and in the end I defined liquidity preference as above for general exposition, making the further distinction between inactive and active demand when required.

(Keynes [1937] 1973, 14: 223)

The inconsistency that arises in the way in which Keynes uses the term liquidity preference might be due to a tension between his intuitive understanding of his theory and his attempt to formalize it. His intuitive understanding told him that the interest rate could be driven by the uncertain expectations and insecurities of wealth-holders. His Marshallian training, however, urged him to attempt to capture that intuition in a demand–supply equilibrium condition. Although there is nothing in the equilibrium condition that is inconsistent with his intuition, it obscures what is interesting and original in Keynes' thinking on the matter.

Practically all interest rate theorists are willing to admit that the interest rate on money loans is determined by the demand for money, either to hold or to borrow, relative to the supply. This is common ground. The area of contention surrounds the question of what lies behind the demand: what kind of factors explain the level of interest that emerges (Haberler [1939] 1958: 206). The orthodox theorists believed the ultimate factors were productivity and thrift. Keynes broke from them in claiming that it was something altogether different – liquidity preference defined broadly as a desire on the part of wealth-holders for flexibility. However, by deciding in the end to define liquidity preference as the demand for money, Keynes failed to communicate what was distinctive about his theory.

It might have been the realization that he had not adequately captured his intuitive understanding of the determination of the interest rate in his supply and demand for money framework that prompted him to write his elusive Chapter 17.

CHAPTER 17 OF THE *GENERAL THEORY*

Chapter 17 presents something of a stumbling block for the reader of Keynes' *General Theory*. It does not mesh well with the rest of the book and its insights are not easily incorporated into the formal model that can be distilled out of the other chapters. The initial title Keynes gave to Chapter 17 suggests he recognized that he was operating at a different level of analysis. Before shortening it to 'The Essential Properties of Interest and Money', he had titled it 'Philosophical Considerations on the Essential Properties of Capital, Interest and Money' ([c. 1934] 1973, 13: 424). The chapter is undoubtedly muddled and it appears that Keynes was grasping at ideas that he had not successfully sorted through in his own mind. About an early draft, he wrote to a reader:

I admit the obscurity of this chapter. A time may come when I am, so to speak, sufficiently familiar with my own ideas to make it easier. But at present I doubt if the chapter is of any use except to someone who has entered into, and is sympathetic with, the ideas in previous chapters.

(Keynes [1935] 1973, 13: 519)

Even after the *General Theory* was published, Keynes was not entirely happy with his exposition of the ideas in Chapter 17. He wrote to another correspondent four months after publication:

You are quite right that the chapters on liquidity premium do not carry matters to their final destination. That is a point about which I have been thinking a good deal since the book was out, and I am already conscious of some important improvements which could be made. But I do still feel that the idea itself provides the clue.

(Keynes [1936] 1979: 213–14)

Many interpreters of Keynes take the position advanced by Hansen (1953: 155) that Chapter 17 of the *General Theory* represents a 'detour which could be omitted without sacrificing the main argument'. But Keynes' efforts to improve what he had written after the book was published and his statement that the idea of a liquidity premium 'provides the clue' suggest that Chapter 17 might be more important than his interpreters have previously thought.

One of the more confusing aspects of Keynes' exposition is the idea of own-rates of interest that he had borrowed from Sraffa. An own-rate of interest is the rate of exchange between a present good and a like future good. For example, if 1.1 future apples exchange for 1 present apple, the own-rate on apples in terms of apples is 10 per cent. Keynes begins by stating that in equilibrium all own-rates of interest measured in terms of a common numeraire will be equal. He then goes on to ask what determines the level at which they equalize. Very few markets exist, however, in which present goods exchange for future goods of the same type. The implication is that most of the own-rates that Keynes discusses are not actual prices and it is not clear what conclusions can be drawn from an analysis of the determination of prices that do not actually exist.

Keynes (1936: 225–7) identifies three attributes that determine an asset's own-rate of interest. They are (1) its yield or net output; (2) its liquidity premium, that is, the amount one is willing to pay for the 'power of disposal' over an asset during a period which may offer a 'potential convenience or security'; (3) its carrying costs entering as a negative term; and (4) its expected appreciation. These attributes can be measured in terms of the asset itself, in which case its expected rate of appreciation will be zero, or in terms of any other good.

Keynes explains how these attributes operate in different degrees for different goods. He says that for capital goods and durable consumer goods, the yield is the predominant component of the own-rate. For non-durable goods, carrying costs are the most significant factor. And, for money, 'its yield is *nil*, and its carrying costs [are] negligible but its liquidity premium [is] substantial' (Keynes 1936: 226). However, the claim that the own-rate on money is determined almost wholly by its liquidity premium is problematic. Robertson ([1935] in Keynes 1973, 13: 509) objected that money earns a yield when it is lent out to finance productive investments, so that it is incorrect to attribute its own-rate solely to its liquidity premium. Another problem with identifying the own-rate on money with its liquidity premium is that it appears to amount to an assertion of what Keynes wants to prove; namely, that the liquidity premium on money determines the rate of interest we observe in the money loan market.

Keynes goes on to argue that wealth-holders will demand those assets with the highest own-rates. If a particular type of capital good is highly profitable, for instance, wealth-holders will substitute out of assets with lower rates of return and into the capital good. But as the demand for the good is felt, its production will increase, the scarcity of whatever it produces is reduced and its profitability declines. A similar result holds true for non-reproducible goods. If a new use for swampland is found, for example, increasing its rate of return, then the demand for it on the part of wealth-holders will raise its price and cause its rate of return to fall.

After noting the market tendencies for the yields on various types of assets to fall, Keynes addresses the question of what sets the brake on their decline – in other words, why they do not fall to zero. The question is reminiscent of Böhm-Bawerk ([1912]

1959), Schumpeter ([1911] 1961), and more recently Kirzner (1990) and it alerts us to the possibility that Keynes' analysis in Chapter 17 has its roots in the thinking he had done about productivity of capital explanations of interest. His discovery (Keynes [1937] 1973, 14: 212) that productivity explanations of interest are circular, is linked to the insight that market processes should erase any surplus arising when the value of the output of a production process is greater than the value of the input. One cannot say that interest exists because of the surplus because the surplus would not exist unless there was interest. The inclusion of the word capital in the earlier version of the chapter title is further evidence that his thinking about the relationship between the productivity of capital and the rate of interest was influential in shaping the ideas in Chapter 17.

Keynes reaches the conclusion that it is the liquidity premium on money that sets the brake on the declining own-rates of interest. Money, he argues, is different from other assets in having an own-rate that is not bid down by market forces. The reasons he gives are his two Essential Properties of Money. The first, the negligible elasticity of production of money, is easy to understand. If a reproducible good has a higher than normal rate of return, then the incentive is there for more of it to be produced. If video-camcorders can be rented out at exorbitant rates, a high demand by entrepreneurs will lead to more being produced in the market, and to a subsequent reduction in their own-rate. If a high rate of return can be made by lending out money, on the other hand, private producers cannot respond by increasing its supply.

The second essential property of money – its negligible elasticity of substitution – is less obvious. The idea is that with other assets the rate of return is usually independent of the asset's price. Take, for example, a second-hand table that Smith buys for $500. Uninterested in speculating on its possible future appreciation as an antique, he buys it merely for the table services it yields, which he values at $50 a year, say. The table's rate of return to Smith, then, is 10 per cent a year. Now suppose Jones sees the table in Smith's home, speculates that it might be a collector's item and offers Smith $1000. In this case, the market price of the table has doubled and its rate of return to Smith falls to 5 per cent. At this point, Smith would be rational to sell the table and substitute it with a cheaper one that yields the same value in table services. When the rate of return on such an asset changes there is an incentive to substitute into or away from it.

Similarly with a capital asset. If the price of camcorders doubles so that a video rental store finds a higher rate of return can be got on renting movies than on renting camcorders, it will invest in more of the former and less of the latter. With money, however, the situation is different. If the value of my cash holdings increases, the value of their liquidity premium will also increase. Suppose my savings consist of $500 and the liquidity premium I attach to them is $50, or 10 per cent per year. Now suppose all prices suddenly drop by 50 per cent, so that the value of my savings doubles. There is no reason to think that as in the case of Smith's table, the rate of return I derive from my asset will drop to 5 per cent, and cause me to get out of money and into assets with a higher rate of return. The crucial difference is that the value of the liquidity premium is not independent of the value of the money. Keynes believed it is plausible that even when the value of my money balances doubles, I still attach close to a 10 per cent liquidity premium.

It would be wrong to suppose, however, that the liquidity premium is totally unaffected by the value of one's cash balances. The real balance or Pigou effect says that since a greater proportion of my wealth is in the form of cash, the marginal liquidity premium in percentage terms might be somewhat lower. Although Keynes did not discuss the real balance effect explicitly, we cannot be sure he ignored it completely, because if he did he would have had a zero rather than a negligible elasticity of substitution: he provides no other explanation as to why it is negligible rather than zero.

The theory that Keynes presents in Chapter 17 can be summarized by the following propositions: (1) The own-rate of interest on an asset is determined by the sum of its yield, its liquidity premium, and its expected rate of appreciation minus its carrying costs. (2) The own-rate of interest on money is equal to its liquidity premium minus a usually negligible carrying cost. (3) Market forces tend to drive down the own-rates on non-money assets. (4) Because of its unique properties, money has an own-rate that is not driven down in the same degree. (5) The equilibrium rate of interest at which all the own-rates are equal is determined by the own-rate on money, that is, by its liquidity premium.

Keynes' line of reasoning in Chapter 17 is ingenious and highly original but ultimately it is not persuasive. We have already mentioned the problem of knowing what to make of an analysis based on the concept of own-rates of interest which, for most goods, do not exist. And we have mentioned the question-begging character of proposition (2). Yet even if these problems are ignored, there is an additional objection that was raised by Robertson (1937) and by Knight (1941). They begin by registering agreement with the idea that in equilibrium the marginal rates of return on various assets will be equal to the marginal liquidity premium on money. Robertson even traces this idea back to Lavington (1921). The point at which they break from Keynes is in the idea that the liquidity premium is the sole determinant of the equilibrium level. With other systems of prices, the equilibrium level is determined jointly by the factors lying behind each individual price. Robertson and Knight were not convinced that, in the case of the interest rate, only one factor is important. Robertson could only explain Keynes' position by attributing it to 'a curious inhibition against visualising more than one margin at once' (1937: 431).

A simple example illustrates the difficulty with Keynes' theory. Suppose the rate of return on a particular type of capital good increases, causing wealth-holders to substitute out of other assets and into the capital good. As wealth-holders continue with these substitutions the own-rate on the capital good is brought into line with the own-rates on all the other assets. But if wealth-holders have been substituting out of money, then it is possible that when the equilibrium is reached, their money balances are reduced and the marginal liquidity premium is higher. The final result is a higher level of the interest rate with a higher liquidity premium, and yet one cannot claim that the liquidity premium is the sole, or even chief, determinant of the new level.

Although the line of reasoning Keynes presents in Chapter 17 is ultimately not persuasive, the chapter contains many important insights that could lead towards a more successful account of the liquidity preference theory. It contains, for example, the key elements that might appear in what we called in Chapter 3 an 'essentialist' analysis of the problem of interest. In Chapter 17, Keynes purports to explain the level of interest: he might have been more successful if he had been asking why interest exists, or what constitutes its originating cause. His demonstration that market forces exert a downward tendency on the rate of return on non-money assets could be used to support the argument that these rates of return cannot explain the existence of interest. In the same vein, his discussion of the reasons why the liquidity premium on money is not bid down leads in the direction of the conclusion that the liquidity preference that gives rise to the liquidity premium could be the originating cause of interest. To reach the conclusion that liquidity preference explains the level of interest, however, he needs some additional assumption. One that would help his case is the assumption that the money supply contracts and expands with the demand for it; that is, that the money supply is endogenous. Moore (1988) argues that although an exogenous money supply was assumed in the *General Theory*, other writings indicate that he often thought of the money supply as endogenous. Another assumption that serves the same purpose is the responsiveness postulate that we present in Chapter 4.

THE RESPONSIVENESS POSTULATE IN KEYNES' THEORY

In Chapter 4 we set out an empirical postulate which we argue is the linchpin of a liquidity preference theory of interest. The postulate says that a slight change in the interest rate arising from a change in the real forces of productivity or thrift will typically bring about a response on the part of speculative wealth-holders large enough to wash out any discernible effect of the real force on the interest rate. The plausibility of the postulate depends on the small magnitude in any time period of changes in the demand and supply for loanable funds arising from real forces, relative to changes in the demand and supply arising from speculative trading in the large stock of existing debt. It is related to the interest elasticity of the demand for money but is not identical with it. A high degree of interest elasticity in the demand for money implies that the proportional change in the quantity of money demanded is high relative to a proportional change in the interest rate. A high degree of responsiveness, on the other hand, only requires that the change in the quantity of speculative balances demanded is high relative to the change in the demand for money that caused the initial movement in the interest rate. It need not imply a large proportional change in the demand for money. The result is that while a high elasticity will usually imply a high degree of responsiveness, the converse need not hold true.

In this section, we examine the question of whether the empirical postulate plays a role in Keynes' liquidity preference theory. We find evidence in both the *General Theory* and his later writings that he did, indeed, maintain such a postulate to be true. However, he did not stress it as an important part of his theory of interest and we can find statements in his post-*General Theory* papers whose validity rests on the postulate not holding true.

We might speculate that with the responsiveness postulate we have another example of Keynes' intuition being stronger than his powers of exposition. His acceptance of the postulate might have played a role in his intuitive discovery of the result that liquidity preference determines the level of interest. Yet by the time he came to exposit and to defend his theory, the crucial premise had been forgotten. His neglect of the responsiveness postulate makes him susceptible to the criticism put forward by Robertson (1937) and Knight (1941) that he did not show why the interest rate was determined at only one margin.

As we argue in Chapter 4, the responsiveness postulate is more likely to be true for those economies with a large stock of existing debt relative to the flows of new debt coming onto the market. In the *Treatise on Money*, Keynes indicates that he believed such a situation existed at the time he was writing:

> The decision as to holding bank-deposits or securities relates, not only to the current increment to the wealth of individuals, but also to the whole block of their existing capital. Indeed, since the current increment is but a trifling proportion of the block of existing wealth, it is but a minor element in the matter.
> (Keynes 1930, 1: 41)

In the *General Theory*, the responsiveness postulate surfaces in what is essentially an *obiter dictum* on the operation of monetary policy. He writes:

> In normal circumstances the amount of money required to satisfy the transactions-motive and the precautionary-motive is mainly a resultant of the general activity of the economic system and of the level of money-income. But it is by playing on the speculative-motive that monetary management . . . is brought to bear on the economic system. For the demand for

money to satisfy the former motives is generally irresponsive to any influence except the actual occurrence of a change in the general economic activity and the level of incomes; whereas experience indicates that the aggregate demand for money to satisfy the speculative motive usually shows a continuous response to gradual changes in the interest rate . . . .

(Keynes 1936: 196–7)

He goes on to argue that without wealth-holders behaving in this way, open market operations would be an impractical way of changing the quantity of money. Because speculators exist who will change their level of cash holdings in response to small changes in the interest rate, the central monetary authority does not need to bid interest rates up or down very far to change the total quantity of money.

Beyond this discussion of monetary policy, however, the responsiveness postulate is not mentioned again in the *General Theory*. Nor is it mentioned in the post-*General Theory* article 'Alternative Theories of the Rate of Interest' ([1937] 1973, 14: 201–15) which was written to clarify his theory of interest. It is startling, therefore, to find that Robertson, in his reply to the article, provides a very lucid account of the postulate when summarizing Keynes' position. He writes:

An act of thrift on my part, so I have understood the argument to run, destroys incomes in one place without creating them in another, *since any tendency of the rate of interest to fall through my purchase of securities is checked by the desire of other wealth-holders, at the slightest sign of such a fall, to part with their securities in exchange for my money.*

(Robertson 1937: 434–5, emphasis added)

It is possible that although the postulate was not clearly spelt out in Keynes' written work, it had entered into his extensive oral discussions with Robertson. We might also note that Robertson did not dispute the postulate and, on the contrary, admitted that it was a line of reasoning to which he has been at 'pains to make guarded concessions' (Robertson 1937: 435). The fact that one of Keynes' harshest and most discerning critics had no problem with the postulate may provide the explanation as to why Keynes had not done much either to explain or to defend it. In presenting a theory as original and controversial as the one presented in the

General Theory, it makes sense that Keynes would not labour points that had already gained acceptance.

Further evidence that the responsiveness postulate was familiar, at least to economists in Cambridge, can be found in Kahn's comments on a draft of what was to become Keynes' famous 1937 *QJE* article.

My only criticism is that the passages about uncertainty fail to connect up with the rest, except that they explain why inactive balances exist. In particular there is nothing . . . to explain why the hypothesis of a calculable future would, if legitimate, result in full employment. I suppose you have in mind that the liquidity preference curve would then be enormously inelastic, so that a small e.g. fall in money wages would give rise to a large fall in the rate of interest. But this bridge is missing in your argument.

I always feel in this connection that the 'two views' of the *Treatise* should not be forgotten. Liquidity preference is elastic not only because of uncertainty but because people differ.

(Kahn [1936] in Keynes 1973, 14: 108)

The (presumably amended) passage in Keynes' *QJE* article runs as follows:

If, on the other hand, our knowledge of the future was calculable and not subject to sudden changes, it might be justifiable to assume that the liquidity-preference curve was both stable and very inelastic. In this case a small decline in money income would lead to a large fall in the rate of interest, probably sufficient to raise output and employment to the full. In these conditions we might reasonably suppose that the whole of the available resources would normally be employed; and the conditions required by the orthodox theory would be satisfied.

(Keynes [1937] 1973, 14: 119)

In another article pursuing the same theme, he writes:

the two elasticities named above [in the desire to hold inactive balances and in the supply of output as a whole] are highly characteristic of the real world; and the assumption that both of them are zero assumes away three-quarters of the problems in which we are interested.

(Keynes [1937] 1973, 14: 107–8)

Possibly because of the prompting he received from Kahn, Keynes was led, in some of his later articles, to emphasize that the responsiveness in the demand for money on the part of wealth-holders was important in leading to his conclusion that market tendencies need not lead to full employment. In a letter[3] written after the *General Theory* was published, he expresses his new-found awareness of the postulate:

On second thoughts the assumption which I ought to have attributed to the classical economists is not that inactive balances are zero, but that they are inelastic in response to changes in the rate of interest, so that a tendency of the active balances to decline has the effect of lowering the rate of interest by whatever extent is necessary to restore them to their previous figure.

(Keynes [1937] 1979: 258)

Although Keynes made progress towards recognizing that his unemployment equilibrium result requires the postulate that wealth-holders vary their money holdings in response to changes in the interest rate, he did not seem to recognize its crucial role in his liquidity preference theory of interest. His confusion on the issue is revealed in his contribution to the controversy with his critics surrounding the question of whether an increased demand for investment funds will cause the interest rate to rise. If one maintains the responsiveness postulate, the answer should be that unless the change in the demand is abnormally large, wealth-holders can defuse pressure on the interest rate by proportionally small changes in their levels of cash holdings. In a letter to Robertson written in March 1935, he did seem to deny an effect on the interest rate:

The first of your three propositions is the following, 'The rate of interest is the price of the use of loanable funds, hence any cause which raises the curve of expected marginal productivity of loanable funds will tend to raise the rate of interest through increasing the competition of borrowers to obtain the use of loanable funds.' You say this is 'plausible and universally believed'. If you were to substitute 'almost universally' I should agree. But it is precisely this proposition which I am denying. What bothers me is not so much that I should have failed to convince you that it is false, as that I

should have apparently failed to convey to you that I deny it!
(Keynes 1973, 13: 522–3)

And yet in a letter of December 1936, he seems to reverse his position.

I lay stress on the fact that the demand for money depends both on the hoarding motive proper and also on the 'prospect of using more money profitably in investment', if this is measured by the increase in invested funds. It is only to the extent that increased investment requires larger active balances that it reacts on the rate of interest, a reaction which can be prevented by increasing the quantity of money. . . . But the main point is that I not only entirely agree with the important point you set forth . . . but consider myself the inventor of it! I have many pages on the theme that increasing investment involves increasing output and that this kicks back on the rate of interest by draining away more money into the active circulation

(Keynes [1936] 1973, 14: 91)

The ambiguity of his position on the matter is well-illustrated in his introduction of the 'finance motive'. In response to criticism by Ohlin, Keynes admitted that the demand for money to carry out new investment was not properly accounted for in the transactions, speculative, and precautionary motives, so the addition of a fourth motive is necessary. He begins by admitting that the demand for money to satisfy the finance motive can influence the interest rate.

If by 'credit' we mean 'finance', I have no objection at all to admitting the demand for finance as one of the factors influencing the rate of interest. For 'finance' constitutes, as we have seen, an additional demand for liquid cash in exchange for a deferred claim.

(Keynes [1937] 1973, 14: 209–10)

In the same paragraph, however, he draws the following conclusion:

But finance is not the only source of demand for money, and the terms on which it is supplied, whether through the banks or through the new issue market, must be more or less the same as the terms on which other demands for money are supplied. Thus it is precisely the liquidity premium on cash ruling in the market which determines the rate of interest at which finance is obtainable.

(Keynes [1937] 1973, 14: 210)

In saying that the liquidity premium on cash determines the rate of interest at which finance is obtainable, he seems to be contradicting his earlier assertion that the demand for finance can influence the rate of interest. His final conclusion would follow if he maintained the responsiveness postulate, but in that case he would have to admit that in normal circumstances the demand for finance does not have any noticeable effect on the interest rate.

The answer to the question of whether the responsiveness postulate plays a role in Keynes' liquidity preference theory is uncertain. On the one hand, he did maintain that an elasticity in 'the desire to hold inactive balances' was 'highly characteristic of the real world' (Keynes [1937] 1973, 14: 107–8), and he did arrive at a conclusion which cannot be sustained unless the responsiveness postulate holds true. And yet, on the other hand, in neither his presentation nor his subsequent defence of his liquidity preference theory of interest, did he spell out the necessity and the crucial role of the responsiveness postulate.

CONCLUSION

A reading of Keynes' papers and correspondence from the time succeeding the publication of the *General Theory* reveals that he was not happy with his account of the liquidity preference theory and had hoped to revise it (Keynes 1979: 213–14, 263). It seemed to be the exposition of the theory, as opposed to the fundamental ideas underlying it, that dissatisfied him. A few months after publication he wrote, referring to the notion of a liquidity premium, that he 'still believe[s] the idea itself provides the clue'. Almost three years later, however, he was still puzzling over that fundamental idea of a liquidity premium. One of his last letters[4] pertaining to the *General Theory* contains the following passage:

I am rather inclined to associate risk premium with probability strictly speaking, and liquidity premium with what in my *Treatise on Probability* I called 'weight'. An essential distinction is that a risk premium is expected to be rewarded on the average by an increased return at the end of the period. A liquidity premium, on the other hand, is not even expected to be so rewarded. It is a payment, not for the expectation of increased tangible income at the end of the period, but for an increased sense of comfort and confidence during the period.

(Keynes [1938] 1979: 293–4)

The letter suggests that Keynes was moving away from the supply and demand for money formulation of the theory and was working his way towards a theory in which liquidity preference enters as a separate motive for demanding money, and one that could be distinguished from the transactions and finance motives.

The indication in Keynes' writings that he was not happy with the exposition of his interest rate theory in the *General Theory*, but that he continued to believe in liquidity preference as the true explanation, opens an important avenue of inquiry. Although it may be futile to attempt to answer the question of what Keynes would have said had he lived long enough to complete a revision, it is worthwhile to look beyond Keynes' formal models and attempt to root out from other parts of his writings clues to his intuitive understanding of the liquidity preference theory – that is, to look beyond the context of justification into the context of discovery.

Our investigation has yielded a number of insights in that direction. We find with Shackle that the genesis of the idea may have arisen in his study of real world financial markets in his *Treatise on Money*. His close familiarity with the institutional detail of these markets increases the likelihood that he was aware of the empirical relevance of the responsiveness postulate. We also find some direct evidence that the postulate did indeed enter into his thinking. We find that although there is support for the interpretation of liquidity preference as the total demand for money, many passages point towards quite a different inter-pretation. In various places, he suggests it is rather a motivation on the part of wealth-holders linked to their desire for 'an increased sense of comfort and confidence' in an uncertain world. Finally, in Chapter 17, we find evidence that he saw the liquidity premium on money, in contrast to the returns on other assets, to have a unique causal significance in the explanation of interest. We argue that the theory in that chapter can be viewed from our 'essentialist' perspective' of Chapter 3.

Chapter 6

The liquidity preference versus loanable funds debate

Much of the literature that was stimulated by Keynes' presentation of his liquidity preference theory of interest is found in the long-standing liquidity preference versus loanable funds debate. The controversy began immediately after the publication of the *General Theory* in 1936 and continued at a heavy pace into the late 1950s, by which time a resolution, of sorts, had been reached. The debate can be divided into two stages. In the first stage, Keynes argued with his contemporaries in the pages of the *Economic Journal* and in private correspondence. His principal foes were his colleague at Cambridge D.H. Robertson, the Swedish economist Bertil Ohlin, and the civil servant Ralph Hawtrey. Their position was that the liquidity preference theory was nothing more than the already established loanable funds theory, dressed up in different language and with a slightly different emphasis. They maintained that Keynes exaggerated the originality of his contribution, and that he was unable to sustain, on the basis of the theory he presented, his conclusions about the irrelevance of productivity and thrift. Keynes, for his part, denied that the theories were equivalent, insisted he was onto something radically new, and accused the loanable funds theorists of committing the same logical fallacy as the supply-of-saving-demand-for-investment interest rate theorists.

Our analysis of this first stage in the debate leads us to come out mainly on the side of the loanable funds theorists. The debate provides further evidence for the position advanced in Chapter 5 that Keynes did not have a clear understanding of his liquidity preference theory in his own mind. The loanable funds theorists, on the other hand, working from a simple and consistent theory, were able to set the terms of the debate, pounce on the weak spots in Keynes' exposition, and defeat him easily. What we take to be the important and original parts of Keynes' theory of interest were left undiscussed.

The second stage of the debate, which took place mainly in the pages of the American economic journals, involved a completely new set of players and took on a markedly different character. While the earlier debate was characterized by an old-fashioned, intuitive, verbal style of reasoning, the later debate aimed at a greater degree of rigour through its use of mathematical modelling. With this methodological shift, the debate became less confusing and conclusions could be arrived at with greater certainty. However, it is not at all clear that the mathematical interpretations of the liquidity preference and loanable funds theories would have satisfied Keynes and his contemporaries. Hence, it is not clear that the conclusions reached in the later debate have any relevance to its earlier version.

The main issue in the later debate was the question of whether or not the theories are equivalent. What is most striking about the literature on the equivalence question is the lack of agreement on how the theories are to be defined. While most of the participants were working within a general equilibrium framework, they had different ideas on whether the theories were supposed to be static or dynamic, partial or general. As a result, the literature is made up of several incomparable conclusions, each resting on a different interpretation of the theories. The other predominant issue in the later debate was the issue of stocks versus flows. Discussion revolved around two questions. First, is a stock theory preferable to a flow theory for an analysis of the interest rate? Is the liquidity preference theory which is expressed in terms of stocks therefore preferable to the loanable funds theory which is expressed in terms of flows? And second, does a stock theory give different results from a flow theory? We conclude that the stocks versus flows controversy, which absorbed a great deal of attention, did not go very far towards finding a resolution to the liquidity preference versus loanable funds debate.

KEYNES AND HIS CONTEMPORARIES

In the *General Theory*, Keynes sought to refute and to replace with his liquidity preference theory of interest, the theory that the rate of interest is determined by the supply of saving relative to the demand for investment. The controversy that the liquidity preference theory stirred after the *General Theory* was published, however, suggests that Keynes' so-called 'classical theory of interest' might have been a strawman. No one chose to defend it against the liquidity preference theory. Instead, several of Keynes' contemporaries chose to argue that the liquidity preference theory was merely an inferior restatement of the already widely accepted loanable funds theory.

Like Keynes, the loanable funds theorists, who included Haberler ([1939] 1958), Hawtrey (1937a, b), Ohlin (1937a, b), and Robertson (1934, 1937, 1940), had moved beyond the dual treatise conception of economics, according to which the Principles of Value and Distribution are dealt with in one volume and the Principles of Money in another. As with Keynes, their dissatisfaction with the classical theory of interest arose from its location in the volume on Value and Distribution, where it is unable to incorporate the effects of monetary phenomena like changes in the money supply or in the propensity to hoard. The loanable funds theorists recognized that monetary factors were important in both the short and the long run. As a result, they could not see how Keynes' theory of interest expressed in terms of the demand and supply of money to hold at a moment in time, had anything to add to the understanding derived from a loanable funds theory expressed in terms of the demand and supply of funds during a period of time.

In a loanable funds theory one divides time up into accounting periods during which a flow of loanable funds is supplied and a corresponding flow is demanded. Robertson (1940) presents a theory in which the supply of loanable funds consists of:

1 current savings effected during the period;
2 disentanglings, that is, savings made in the past, released from embodiment in fixed or working capital;
3 net dishoardings; and
4 net additional bank loans.

While the demand for loanable funds consists of:

1 funds destined for expenditure on building up new increments of fixed or working capital;
2 funds destined for maintenance or replacement of existing fixed or working capital;

3 funds destined to be put in store; and
4 funds destined for expenditure on consumption whether individual or collective.

The interest rate is then supposed to be determined by the interaction of demand and supply in the usual way. Any factor increasing the supply has a depressing influence on the interest rate, while any factor increasing the demand causes the interest rate to rise. The loanable funds theorists maintained that if one were to consider the effect of the same factors within the context of a demand and supply for money theory, one would get equivalent results. Robertson, for example, writes:

> I nourish a hope that [Keynes] will yet come to agree that analysis in terms of supply and demand for money-to-hold for a moment of time, and analysis in terms of supply and demand for money-to-lend during an interval of time, are *alternative* methods of procedure; and that, while neither is more than a first stage in the elucidation of the underlying forces governing the rate of interest, either, *if carried through consistently* will give the same result as the other.
>
> (Robertson 1940: 317)

Keynes' position on whether or not the two theories give identical results is not clear. On the one hand, he responded to a demonstration by Hicks (1936) that the two theories are equivalent by asking:

> I am not clear what you mean by 'the demand and supply for loans'. Do you mean the demand and supply for loans *in terms of money*? If so, what is the crucial point in which this departs from my treatment? It looks to me to be the same thing over again.
>
> (Keynes [1936] 1973, 14: 75)

And yet at other times he was to say that the loanable funds theory was 'fundamental heresy' (Keynes [1937] 1973: 185) which was 'radically opposed' (ibid.: 202) to his own theory. On still other occasions, Keynes claimed not to understand the loanable funds theory (ibid.: 81, 92). His claim is surprising because the theory is not difficult. The trouble seemed to be that he was convinced that the supply-of-saving-demand-for-investment theory was logically flawed and sensed that a theory such as the one that the loanable funds theorists were presenting, in which the old theory is modified by tacking on monetary factors, must be similarly flawed. Keynes seemed to be making a presumption of guilt by association and never provided a thorough critique of the loanable funds theory, as such. His only direct criticism was of a statement of the theory by Ohlin. Keynes ([1937] 1973, 14: 203–6) focussed all his criticism on one comment that Ohlin was later to retract, and which therefore cannot be considered central to the loanable funds theory.

Keynes did give his endorsement to a critique of the loanable funds theory made by Lerner (1938). He described Lerner's article as being 'clear as daylight' (Keynes [1938] 1979: 281), saying that it 'expresses views which I share' (ibid.: 271). Lerner bases his critique on a version of the loanable funds theory that says the supply of loanable funds is equal to the flow of new savings within a given period plus the supply of newly created money; while the demand for loanable funds is equal to the demand for investment within a period plus the demand for additional hoards. He argues that if at the equilibrium rate of interest the supply of new money is different from the demand for additional hoards, then the amount of investment will be different from the amount of saving. The result is anomalous, since by definition the amount of investment is always equal to the amount of saving.

The flaw in Lerner's argument is that it fails to make the distinction between the demand for investment *funds* and the demand for investment *goods* that those funds are destined to buy. It is the demand for investment *funds* that belongs on the demand side of the loanable funds equation, but it is the value of the demand for investment *goods* that is equal to the quantity of savings. Consider a specific example. Suppose within a given period, the demand for investment funds is equal to X and there is dishoarding by exactly the same amount. Further, suppose there is no saving and no new money being created. The demand for loanable funds nets out at zero and is equal to the supply. We have a situation in which the demand for investment funds is greater than the supply of saving. However, as soon as those investment funds are spent, saving – defined as the excess of income over consumption – increases by the same amount.[1]

It is surprising that Keynes found no flaw in Lerner's argument and rather gave it whole-hearted endorsement, because in an article published the previous year, Keynes ([1937]

1973, 14: 215–23) admitted that he had neglected but now recognized the importance of the distinction that we have just drawn between the demand for investment funds and the demand for investment goods. He labelled the former *ex ante* investment and admitted its role in the determination of the interest rate. And he recognized the latter, which he called *ex post* investment, as the amount that always brings with it an equal amount of saving and thus which will not affect the interest rate.[2]

Keynes provided no convincing reason why the loanable funds theorists should give up their theory and replace it with the liquidity preference theory. The loanable funds theorists believed the liquidity preference theory should give equivalent results but remained firmly attached to their procedure because they thought Keynes' formulation obscured the role of the real factors of productivity and thrift. Robertson's objection to the liquidity preference theory was that its lack of attention to real factors leads to a kind of bootstrap argument. He writes:

> While there are hints here and there of a broader treatment, in the main [Keynes'] plan is to set the rate of interest in a direct functional relation only with that part of the money stock which is held for what he calls 'speculative reasons', i.e., because it is expected that the rate of interest will subsequently rise. Thus the rate of interest is what it is because it is expected to become other than it is; if it is not expected to become other than it is, there is nothing left to tell us why it is what it is. The organ which secretes it has been amputated, and yet it somehow still exists – a grin without a cat . . . . If we ask what ultimately governs the judgments of wealth-owners as to why the rate of interest should be different in the future from what it is to-day, we are surely led straight back to the fundamental phenomena of Productivity and Thrift.
>
> (Robertson 1940: 25)

Ohlin complained that the liquidity preference theory does not integrate the theory of interest with the theory of prices. He writes that his own theory agrees with equilibrium theory

> and differs from Keynes' construction in one essential respect: it brings out the relation of the rates of interest to the other elements of the price system and to their movements, whereas Keynes' construction – unless it is interpreted in a way which

he probably does not accept – seems to regard the rates of interest as determined largely 'outside' the price system.

(Ohlin 1937b: 227)

The loanable funds theorists were justified in complaining that Keynes' liquidity preference theory did not make clear the role of non-monetary factors. We have already discussed in Chapter 5 Keynes' vacillation on the question of whether a change in the demand for investment will have an effect on the interest rate. Initially, thinking that a change in the amount of investment spending always brings with it an equal sized change in the amount of saving, Keynes denied any effect. Later, in response to a comment by Ohlin, he was to recognize (Keynes [1937] 1973, 14: 215–23) that while a change in investment spending might bring with it a change in saving, investment borrowing *per se* does not necessitate any change in the amount of saving. And, since it is the borrowing that first plays a role in the loanable funds market, at least a temporary effect on the interest rate is possible.

The loanable funds theorists thought that in making this concession, Keynes was readmitting the influence of productivity through a back door (Robertson 1936: 182). A fundamental difference remains, however. Keynes was allowing only a short-run effect on the interest rate resulting from the lag between the entrepreneurs' securing of funds and their spending them. Once the funds are spent, he believed, the movement in the interest rate would reverse itself. The loanable funds theorist, on the other hand, was inclined to believe that productivity was one of the determining factors in the long-run (Robertson [1936] in Keynes 1973, 14: 97–8).

Keynes vacillated less on the question of the role of saving in the determination of the interest rate. His strongest statement on the matter was:

the transition from a lower to a higher scale of activity involves an increased demand for liquid resources which cannot be met without a rise in the rate of interest, unless the banks are ready to lend more cash or the rest of the public to release more cash at the existing rate of interest. If there is no change in the liquidity position, the public can save *ex ante* and *ex post* and *ex* anything else until they are blue in the face, without alleviating the problem in the least – unless, indeed, the result of their efforts is to lower the scale of activity to what it was before . . . .

The investment market can become congested through a shortage of cash. It can never become congested through shortage of saving.

(Keynes [1937] 1973, 14: 222)

By this statement Keynes suggests that if there is an increase in the demand for investment funds, an increase in the propensity to save will not succeed in meeting it. What is necessary is not more saving, but more cash. Keynes seems to fail to recognize, however, that more saving will always imply more cash to lend, unless the whole of the new saving is hoarded. His thinking that saving and cash are two distinct entities is also revealed in his complaint about the supply of loanable funds that it is 'some sort of hotch-potch between cash and saving' (Keynes [1938] 1973, 14: 229). Possibly because of his complete rejection of the supply-of-saving-demand-for-investment theory of interest, Keynes was reluctant to allow saving any role in the determination of the interest rate. Yet it is obvious that if people decide to save more, less cash is necessary to satisfy the transactions motive and thus, assuming no change in the propensity to hoard, there will be more cash available for lending.

One possible explanation is that while the loanable funds theorists thought in terms of processes through time, Keynes tended to think in terms of static 'snapshots' (Johnson 1951–2). In Keynes' scheme, an increase in the propensity to save will cause incomes to fall and thus may mean that by the beginning of the next period, the amount of saving is unchanged. Keynes was inclined to jump to the beginning of the next period and thus conclude no effect on the loanable funds market from a change in the propensity to save. The loanable funds theorists, on the other hand, were looking at the process throughout the period and thus concluded there would be an effect.[3]

With almost every major issue in the debate between Keynes and his contemporaries on the question of liquidity preference versus loanable funds, Keynes appeared to be in the weaker position. He maintained that the theories are 'radically opposed' and yet he gave no reason why they should give different results. Both Keynes' liquidity preference theory and the loanable funds theory agree on the question of the market in which the interest rate is determined. The differences are only in their formal structure. First, Keynes employs an analysis in terms of stocks at a moment in time, while the loanable funds theorist looks at flows through a period of time. Second, there is a difference in how the various elements that enter into the market are categorized. Keynes incorporates into the demand side all the elements except for the exogenously determined supply of money. The loanable funds theorists, on the other hand, include on the supply side of the loanable funds equation the flow of saving in addition to the changes in the supply of money. For example, if people substitute bonds with increased transactions balances, then in Keynes' theory there will be an outward shift in the demand for money, while in the loanable funds theory, the change will be represented as a decrease in saving, and hence by an inward shift of the supply of loanable funds. Both theories, however, would predict a rise in the rate of interest.

A second issue in the debate was Keynes' ([1937] 1973, 14: 205–6) insistence that the loanable funds theory shares the same logical defect as the supply-of-saving-demand-for-investment theory. We argue in the previous chapter that the only defect in the classical theory that Keynes was able to prove was that it ignored monetary factors – a defect which the loanable funds theorists had clearly amended. Using as an excuse the claim that he did not understand the loanable funds theory, Keynes never gave the theory the benefit of a serious critique, and thus failed to convince the loanable funds theorists of any error in their thinking.

A final issue in the liquidity preference versus loanable funds debate was the question of whether Keynes had properly accounted for the effect of changes in saving and investment on the interest rate. We argue that on this issue the loanable funds theorists were justified in their criticism of Keynes. Keynes' emphasis on the necessary equality of saving and investment led him to believe wrongly that they could have no effect on the loanable funds market. Within the course of the debate he equivocated on the question of the role of investment but continued to deny any effect of saving.

As frameworks for analysis the liquidity preference and the loanable funds theories should give equivalent results. That is not to say, however, that Keynes' work in the theory of interest adds nothing to what could be found in the existing loanable funds theories. The real differences between the two sides lay in the more substantive issue of the nature of the market processes through which equilibrium is reached in the loanable funds market and the resulting conclusions about the significance of the various elements that enter into the market. The loanable funds theorists would conclude that the factors of productivity and thrift are important, while Keynes reached his result that the liquidity preferences of wealth-holders are of overwhelming significance. Had the two sides in the debate been able to agree on a conceptual framework, then these substantive issues might have been discussed, and a more fruitful debate would have emerged. Unfortunately, Keynes' inability to give a clear account of his own framework and his refusal to come to grips with the loanable funds theory meant that the two sides never reached any common ground from which to proceed.

THE LATER DEBATE: THE EQUIVALENCE QUESTION

The liquidity preference versus loanable funds controversy continued in the literature long after the original players had ceased to participate. The later debate, however, took on a markedly different character. Although the later participants believed their discussion had its roots in the controversy between Keynes and his colleagues, the connection between the two debates is often difficult to discern. On a superficial level, it would seem the difference was that the later economists were aiming at a greater degree of rigour in their analysis. With few exceptions, arguments were presented in the form of mathematical models within the context of a general equilibrium framework. But the choice of a general equilibrium framework led to a subtle shift in the interpretation of the theories. The early economists did not employ the framework in their original expositions so it is not at all clear that the interpretations of the later economists were the intended ones. The implicit assumption of the later economists was that the verbal theories of their predecessors had a direct mathematical analogue within the general equilibrium model that could be employed to clarify the earlier muddled controversy. Looking back on the earlier debate in the light of the later one, however, one senses two different controversies by the same name.

The major issue in the later debate was the question of whether the two theories give equivalent results. The main contributors to this aspect of the debate were Hicks (1936, 1939), Fellner and

Somers (1941), Lerner (1944), Klein (1950a, b), Hahn (1955), Tsiang (1956), Ackley (1957) and Patinkin (1958). Discussion of the issue was somewhat disjointed because each participant was inclined to offer his own definition of the two theories, and then to proceed on the basis of this to argue for or against equivalence. Given his definition, each contributor's conclusion followed logically and was left undisputed. It would seem, then, that the real issue was not whether the liquidity preference and loanable funds theories are equivalent, but which was the most appropriate interpretation of the theories.

The starting point for the later discussion on the equivalence question can be traced back to a demonstration of equivalence made by Hicks in his 1936 review article of the *General Theory*, and which he later repeated in *Value and Capital* (1939). Although by dates Hicks should be classified within the early debate, his style of reasoning shares a greater affinity with the participants in the later one. Moreover, although Keynes read the 1936 article, neither he nor the loanable funds theorists discussed Hicks' equivalence demonstration in the course of their debate. The explanation is probably that they did not see its relevance.

Hicks' result follows quite simply from the definitions that he attaches to the two theories. Recognizing that to determine the prices of n goods in a general equilibrium system one needs only $n-1$ excess demand equations, Hicks defines the liquidity preference theory as a general equilibrium model in which the excess demand equation for loans has been eliminated. Similarly, a loanable funds theory is construed as a general equilibrium model in which the excess demand equation for money has been eliminated.

The ordinary method of economic theory would be to regard each price as determined by the demand and supply equation for the corresponding commodity or factor; the rate of interest as determined by the demand and supply for loans. If we work in this way, the equation for the demand and supply of money is otiose – it follows from the rest . . . . But we could equally well work in another way. We could allot to each commodity or factor the demand and supply equation for that commodity or factor, as before; but we could allot to the rate of interest the equation for the demand and supply of money. If we do this, the equation for loans becomes otiose, automatically following from the rest . . . .

This latter method is the method of Mr Keynes. It is a perfectly legitimate method, but it does not prove other methods to be wrong.

(Hicks 1936: 246)

Hicks' reasoning may be sound but his interpretation of what the liquidity preference and loanable funds theories have to say, is suspect. Keynes and his contemporaries were not working within the context of a general equilibrium framework in which the demand and supply of each good is considered in terms of all other goods. Rather, their analysis focussed on the single market in which money is exchanged for deferred claims on money, and the influences from other markets were considered only insofar as they operated through that single market. That is not to say, however, that they were employing a partial equilibrium model in the strict sense of the term. A partial equilibrium model is merely a general equilibrium model with the prices of all other goods taken as given. The analyses of the earlier theorists, however, are flexible enough to incorporate the effect of changing prices in other markets.

Even if one accepts the general equilibrium framework as appropriate for the theories, another problem with Hicks' interpretation remains. The problem is that to eliminate the excess demand equation for money does not imply that the interest rate is 'determined' by the excess demand equation for bonds, or *vice versa*. As Hahn (1955: 53) argues: 'In a general equilibrium analysis . . . all prices are 'determined' by all supply-and-demand relations simultaneously, in the sense that we need all of these to find the equilibrium price.' Lerner effectively raised this issue when he asked, in response to Hicks' demonstration, what kind of interest rate theory one would have if one eliminated the equation for peanuts.

Yet despite the obvious limitations of Hicks' characterization of the liquidity preference-loanable funds controversy,[4] it had an important impact in shaping the discussion that was to come; and it is still believed by some authorities to capture the main issue in the debate. Patinkin, for example, writes that

the pointless and depressing 'liquidity-preference *versus* loanable-funds' debate that was to drag on in the literature for years . . . stemmed largely from Keynes' failure to adopt the appropriate general-equilibrium view of his own theory . . . .

As is well known, the futility of this debate had already been demonstrated in Hicks's 1936 review article.

(Patinkin 1976: 140)

A second attempt to demonstrate the equivalence of the two theories was made by Fellner and Somers (1941). They present their own slightly different interpretation of the debate. They define the two theories as both being partial equilibrium theories in which one assumes that the prices of all goods and services, except for money and bonds, are given. They assert that the liquidity preference theory says that the interest rate is determined by the total demand for money in relation to its supply. The total demand for money is made up of three parts: (1) L_a, the part corresponding to the goods and services (excluding money and bonds) that are being put up for sale, (2) L_b, the part corresponding to the money balances that people have decided to hold on to, that is, their reservation demand, and (3) L_c, the part corresponding to the bonds that are being put up for sale. Similarly, the supply of money is divided into three parts: (1) M_a, the part corresponding to the demand for goods and services (again excluding money and bonds), (2) M_b, the part corresponding to the supply of one's own money, and (3) M_c, the part corresponding to the demand for bonds. Fellner and Somers go on to argue that in a partial equilibrium interpretation $L_a = M_a$ regardless of the interest rate: the markets for goods and services are assumed to clear independently of the markets for bonds and money. They are assuming a classical dichotomy where instead of simply separating the supply and demand for money equation from the real sector, they are also separating the supply and demand for bonds equation. Moreover, they argue that $L_b = M_b$ regardless of the interest rate because they are equal by definition. The conclusion they draw is that the liquidity preference theory is reduced to saying that the interest rate is determined by the demand and supply for bonds, which they interpret to be the loanable funds theory. Hence the equivalence of the two theories.

Their analysis raises the question of what good the bonds are traded for. If they are traded for money, then the loanable funds theory reduces to Keynes' version of the liquidity preference theory, simply by definition. Keynes had defined his theory as saying that interest is determined by the demand and supply of money *in terms of bonds*. In Fellner and Somers' scheme, however, the definitional equivalence of the theories does not hold because their liquidity preference theory refers to the demand and supply of money in terms of all other goods, not just in terms of bonds. Thus, when the baker supplies a loaf of bread on the market, he is thought to be demanding money, and this demand is thought to have an effect on the interest rate. While the interpretation of the liquidity preference theory taken by Fellner and Somers is true to the general equilibrium framework that they are employing, it is a clear departure from Keynes.

Lerner (1944) shows that liquidity preference is equivalent to loanable funds by reformulating the loanable funds theory in order to remedy what he perceives to be its crucial flaw. He identifies the problem with the loanable funds theory as being that the supply and demand curves for loans are interdependent: a shift in one implies a shift in the other. The reasoning is that a shift in either curve will bring about a change in income which will shift the other. An increase in the demand for investment funds, for example, will lead to a higher degree of investment spending, a higher level of income, and thus a shift in the supply of savings. Lerner neglects to explain, however, how the increase in the demand for investment funds will be satisfied. It cannot lead, in itself, to a higher level of income unless the funds come from some source of supply. The loanable funds theorists would conceive of a movement up the supply curve as suppliers save more, hoard less, or do both in response to an increased interest rate. The extent of an increased level of income would depend on the relative magnitude of dishoarding relative to new saving and its effect would be taken into consideration in the next period. Just as in his earlier article (Lerner 1938), he collapses the shift in the demand for loanable funds and the spending of those funds into one moment of time. Greater clarity is achieved, however, by considering one step at a time.

In his equivalence demonstration, Lerner suggests that the defect in the loanable funds theory can be remedied by only considering the demand for loanable funds 'which the borrowers, or the other people who indirectly receive the borrowed money, wish to add to their stock of cash' (Lerner 1944: 89). Similarly with the supply, one should consider only those funds which come from new issues of cash or from dishoardings. He goes on:

If we add the stock of cash actually in existence to both sides of this supply and demand, and subtract the decrease in the demand for cash from both sides (i.e. the cash set free and loaned out, directly or indirectly), we have the demand for loans translated into the demand for cash and the supply of loans translated into the supply of cash.

(Lerner 1944: 90)

Lerner's equivalence proof has an *ad hoc* character. Akin to Samuelson's solution to the Marxian transformation problem, it seems to amount to erasing the loanable funds equation and writing in its place the liquidity preference equation. The clue to understanding his method is his contention (unstated in the 1944 article but clear from his 1938 piece) that the parts of the demand for and supply of loanable funds that he neglects are identically equal and thus make no difference to the matter. However, as Tsiang (1956) and others were later to point out, it is only the *ex post* values that are identically equal, the *ex ante* values have a role to play.

In his 1950 *Econometrica* article, Klein offers yet another inter-pretation of what the two theories say and his own conclusion about whether they are equivalent. Realizing that within the context of a static general equilibrium model it makes no sense to ask which one equation 'determines' the rate of interest, he presents instead a dynamic interpretation. A liquidity preference theory, he asserts, is a theory that says the interest rate will adjust if and only if the excess demand for money is different from zero. In a similar vein, a loanable funds theory says that the interest rate will adjust if and only if the excess demand for bonds is different from zero. By setting out an aggregative general equilibrium model, he shows that given his interpretation, the two theories do not give equivalent results. The condition that the interest rate shifts only when the excess demand for money is different from zero, does not imply that it will shift only when the excess demand for bonds is different from zero. Through algebraic manipulation of his model, he shows that under his interpretation of the liquidity preference theory, the interest rate can shift even when there is an equilibrium in the bond market.

Again, as with Fellner and Somers' definition of the liquidity preference theory, one senses that the Klein interpretation does not accord with what Keynes had originally intended. Keynes and his contemporaries were thinking of a loanable funds market in which bonds exchange for money. Disequilibrium on one side of the market would imply disequilibrium on the other. Within a general equilibrium scheme, on the other hand, it is possible that people are holding exactly the amount of bonds that they desire and that an excess demand for money is matched by an excess supply of shoes, say. The price of shoes in terms of money is too high to clear the market. According to the Klein interpretation of the liquidity preference theory, a change in the interest rate is predicted. It is not clear from Keynes' presentation of the liquidity preference theory, however, that he would predict a change in the interest rate arising out of disequilibrium in the market in which money exchanges for shoes.

Fellner and Somers find implausible Klein's result that the interest rate can change even when the bond market is in equilibrium.

It is true, of course, that in a multidimensional system there are a great many factors that affect the interest rate. However, in *any* system, these factors can affect the market rate of interest only through their effect on the demand and supply of interest-bearing securities.

(Fellner and Somers 1950a: 244)

But the only reason Fellner and Somers did not obtain the same result from their model was that they assumed all the markets except for the bond and money markets were in equilibrium. Since they were working with the same general equilibrium framework as was Klein, they would have to admit that if the bond market was in equilibrium but the market in which shoes exchange for money was out of equilibrium, then under their interpretation of the liquidity preference theory as well, the interest rate would change.

Brunner also sensed a problem with Klein's result:

It strains our imagination to think of a change in price of a specific commodity because of disequilibria in other markets of the system, without the necessity of first breaking up the market equilibrium of the commodity under consideration.

(Brunner 1950: 251)

Klein, however, did not think the result that the interest rate can change when the bond market is in equilibrium presented any real problem and, on the contrary, thought that to be worried about it 'closes the door to scientific discussion'. He writes:

> The dogmatic assertion of Fellner and Somers that ' . . . in *any* system, these factors [other than the demand and supply of securities] can affect the market rate of interest only through their effect on the demand and supply of interest-bearing securities' closes the door to scientific discussion. This is, self-evidently, the central assumption of the loanable funds theory, but it cannot be used to prove that the liquidity preference theory is identical . . . .
>
> (Klein 1950b: 246)

Hahn (1955) presents yet another interpretation of the liquidity preference theory. He attempts to bring the interpretation of liquidity preference into closer accord with what Keynes had intended. Hence he asserts that liquidity preference is better expressed as the ratio of money to bonds that people wish to hold rather than simply as the absolute quantity of money that people wish to hold. Adapting Klein's (1950a) interpretation, the liquidity preference theory is construed to say that the interest rate will change if and only if the ratio in which money and bonds are demanded is different from the ratio in which they are supplied. The loanable funds theory says that the interest rate will change if and only if the excess demand for bonds is different from zero. Hahn writes down two equilibrium conditions: the first is that the excess demand for assets is zero and the second is that the ratio of bonds to money demanded is equal to the ratio in which they are supplied. If the first equilibrium condition holds, then for the second not to hold implies that the excess demand for bonds does not equal zero. Thus when *ex ante* saving equals *ex ante* investment, that is, when the first equilibrium condition holds, then the liquidity preference theory is equivalent to the loanable funds theory.

If the first condition does not hold, however, then liquidity preference and loanable funds do not give the same result. Take, for example, a case in which liquidity preference is satisfied, there is a negative excess demand for assets, and a positive excess demand for bonds. In this case the liquidity preference theory predicts no change, while the loanable funds theory does predict a change.

Of all the contributors to the later debate, Tsiang (1956) was the closest in his method to that of the participants in the earlier discussion. His article does much to further Robertson's position in the earlier debate, as Robertson himself acknowledged (Tsiang 1980: 475). Tsiang attempts to replace the previous efforts of Hicks (1936), Fellner and Somers (1941) and Lerner (1944) to prove that the two theories are equivalent. He breaks from these authors in taking the position that:

> To prove convincingly that the two theories are in fact the same, we must demonstrate that the decision on the part of any economic subject, be it a firm or an individual, to demand or supply loanable funds necessarily involves a corresponding decision to hold or part with money.
>
> (Tsiang 1956: 541)

Here Tsiang indicates that he is not so much concerned with the mathematical structure of the model but rather about its content in terms of individual decision making. He defines the liquidity preference theory to say that the interest rate is determined by the demand for money at a moment in time relative to its supply. The loanable funds theory says the interest rate is determined by the demand for a flow of loanable funds within a period relative to the supply within that period. He presents a period model of the type that Robertson (1940) had presented in which time is broken up into small periods that are called days, and he assumes loan contracts are effected at the beginning of the day: 'In this way, we shall be enabled to analyze the dynamic process of changes in income, interest rate, etc., into a series of 'cinematographic' pictures of short-term equilibria at small intervals of time' (Tsiang 1956). He then goes on to show that by dissecting the demand for and supply of loanable funds, they can be seen to be equivalent to the demand for and supply of money.

Tsiang concludes:

> The perfect agreement between the two theories is found to exist because the *ex ante* decisions to supply loanable funds to the market necessarily imply corresponding decisions (also *ex ante*) as to the funds required to finance one's own consumption and one's own demand for idle money, while decisions to take loanable funds off the market necessarily imply corresponding decisions as to the requirements for funds to finance investment expenditures.
>
> (Tsiang 1956: 551)

Tsiang also concludes that the liquidity preference theorists were wrong to assert that changes in thrift and productivity would not affect the interest rate because one can clearly see their effect on the transactions demand for money. He says that

all the disagreements between the loanable funds and liquidity preference theories on practical issues seem to arise from the failure on the part of liquidity preference theorists themselves to perceive the dependence of the aggregate liquidity preference (or demand for money) function upon the consumption and investment functions.

(Tsiang 1956: 555)

Ackley (1957) sets Tsiang's analysis within the context of a more general model and notes that the equivalence only applies when the system is in equilibrium. He notes that in comparing the theories we need to know what kind of assumption is being made with regard to the question of how quickly the actual stock of cash conforms to the desired stock. If the adjustment on the part of speculators is very quick, then it may be completed before the interest rate has a chance to react on saving or investment.

For Ackley, a liquidity preference theory deals with asset-holding equilibrium but the loanable funds theory deals with what happens out of equilibrium. He concludes that only a loanable funds theory is capable of saying something about the speed of adjustment of the desired stock of cash to the actual stock. According to Ackley, in Tsiang's model any excess supply of cash is absorbed by speculators at the beginning of the day. (Since the market must clear at the beginning of the day, not enough time elapses for producers to change their investment spending plans.) Ackley notes that

even with a very moderate interest elasticity of the Keynesian speculative demand schedule (in stock terms), the magnitude and the slope (with respect to the interest rate) of the hoarding–dishoarding component should completely swamp saving and investment in the supply and demand for funds.

(Ackley 1957: 667)

It appears that Ackley is attributing to Tsiang the responsiveness postulate that we present in Chapter 4. It is odd that he should do so, however, since to admit the responsiveness postulate is to admit a minor role to productivity and thrift.

Patinkin (1958) sets out a simple general equilibrium model with four markets: for commodities (C), labour (L), bonds (B), and paper money (M). He assumes for simplicity that the labour market is always in equilibrium. The result is that Walras' Law can be expressed as:

$$M^d - M^s = (C^s - C^d) + (B^s - B^d) \tag{1}$$

Employing the Klein (1950a) specification of the two theories the liquidity preference theory can be described as one in which the adjustment of the interest rate follows:

$$dr/dt = k_1(M^d - M^s) \tag{2}$$

The loanable funds theory similarly can be described as one in which the adjustment of the interest rate follows:

$$dr/dt = k_2(B^d - B^s) \tag{3}$$

In both theories the price adjustment in the commodities market follows:

$$dp/dt = k_3(C^d - C^s) \tag{4}$$

Patinkin proves non-equivalence of the two theories by noting that (2) and (4) give a different dynamic system than (3) and (4). He comes out in favour of a loanable funds theory because equation (2) yields the implausible result that the interest rate can fall due to an excess supply of money even when there is an excess supply of bonds. It is difficult on intuitive grounds to accept that bond prices will rise when there is an excess supply of them. Patinkin has extended Klein's (1950a) result that the interest rate can change when the bond market is in equilibrium, to show more clearly the problem with the liquidity preference theory under Klein's dynamic interpretation.

Patinkin concludes that the theories are not equivalent and that the loanable funds version makes more sense. One has to bear in mind, however, that his results depend on a particular interpretation of the liquidity preference theory and cannot be extended beyond it: for it is not clear that Keynes, or any other defender of the liquidity preference theory, would have endorsed the interpretation.

After Patinkin's contribution, the later debate on the equivalence of liquidity preference with loanable funds died down. A resolution, of sorts, had been reached. In his lecture, 'The General

Theory after Twenty-five Years', Johnson (1961: 7) sums up the debate as concluding that within the static context of a general equilibrium model the two theories are equivalent, but that within the dynamic context, the loanable funds theory 'definitely makes more economic sense'. The question of whether the general equilibrium framework is the appropriate one for the interpretation of the theories is not addressed.

THE LATER DEBATE: STOCKS VERSUS FLOWS

In the early debate, the question of stocks versus flows posed no issue. Both sides recognized that the liquidity preference theory was formulated in terms of stocks and that the loanable funds theory was formulated in terms of flows; but the difference was not considered to be of any importance. In the later debate, however, the stocks versus flows question became a central issue. The debate revolved around two related questions. The first question was whether, in the construction of a theory of the rate of interest, one formulation is preferable to the other. If so, one would have reason to prefer a liquidity preference over a loanable funds theory, or *vice versa*. The second question was whether a theory in terms of stocks is equivalent to one in terms of flows. The latter question is, of course, related to the question of the equivalence of liquidity preference and loanable funds.

Scitovsky (1940) argues that a theory of interest is best formulated in terms of stocks because of the large size of the stock of existing bonds, relative to the flows of bonds coming off and onto the market. He provides a general example of a market for a good that has both a stock and a flow component. He supposes that current production and consumption flows are in equilibrium at the current market price and that this price also equilibrates the supply and demand for stocks. He then supposes a shift, say a fall, in consumer demand for the good. He notes that the price will tend to fall in order to bring the flow schedules into equilibrium. At even a slightly lower price, however, the holders of stocks may want to increase their holdings. Thus, the stockholders' behaviour may counteract the flow adjustment and prevent it from taking place. Scitovsky presents this possibility as reason for expressing a theory of the price of a good for which large stocks exist, in terms of stocks rather than flows. All Scitovsky has convincingly shown, however, is that one should not ignore the existence of stocks when explaining price. He has not shown that a flow theory which pays attention to existing stocks is inadequate. Patinkin writes in defence of flow theory:

I would like to venture the suggestion that all of economic analysis is really concerned with flows and not stocks. For there are two possibilities: either the stock is immutably fixed – and always has been so – in which case there is nothing to analyze; or the stock is subject to variation – in which case this variation constitutes a flow which can be analyzed as such. This and the preceding discussion should point out the *non sequitur* in the contention sometimes advanced that only stock analysis is appropriate for those economic goods whose existing stock is very great in comparison with current production. Clearly, the analysis of any such good can be carried out just as well in terms of the flow of current production – though in this analysis the existing stock will obviously be one of the factors that must be taken into consideration.

(Patinkin 1958: 305)

Others including Lerner (1944) and Fellner and Somers (1949) questioned whether there was any real issue relating to stocks and flows in the interest rate debate. Intuitively, it would seem that if two analysts are looking at the same market and paying attention to the same factors, it should not make any substantive difference to their conclusions whether they frame their statements in terms of stocks at a moment in time or flows through a period of time. As Fellner and Somers argue:

Any infinitesimal period during which members of the public obtain what they want but do not yet possess, and during which they get rid of what they do not want but do possess, must end with a point of time at which they hold precisely what they wish to hold. This is self-evident.

(Fellner and Somers 1949: 146)

Klein (1950a), however, took issue with Fellner and Somers and denied that stock and flow analysis are equivalent. Klein argues that it makes a crucial difference to the results whether one says that a price changes when the excess demand in terms of flows is unequal to zero or whether one says that a price changes when excess demand in terms of stocks is unequal to zero. He shows mathematically that it makes a difference to the time path of the price if the adjustment process is given by a flow equation rather than a stock equation.

A lively exchange ensued in the pages of *Econometrica* between Klein and Fellner and Somers. Through the exchange it was revealed that Fellner and Somers arrived at their conclusion by assuming that stocks were in equilibrium by the end of each hypothetical period. Klein admitted that if this assumption is made, then the stock and flow models give the same results. But he dismissed what Fellner and Somers were doing as 'sham dynamics' and contended that he was giving 'a more realistic picture of economic processes that yields much richer results' (Klein 1950b: 246).

Fellner and Somers (1950) did not give their assumption any defence beyond saying that it is usual procedure and that it is also made by Keynes (1936) and Lerner (1944). They might have defended it, however, on empirical grounds. They could have argued that the market in which bonds exchange for money is highly organized and 'thick' with buyers and sellers at a wide range of prices. The result is that an adjustment of one's actual to desired stock can be made almost instantaneously. Whereas in other markets the assumption that stocks clear in every period might be unrealistic, in the money-bond market it might be a fair representation. Klein was right on the technical point that in a generalized dynamic model, it makes a difference whether the adjustment process is specified in stocks or flows. But Fellner and Somers and others, who intuited that it makes no difference whether one uses stocks or flows, through their implicit assumption that stocks adjust to equilibrium rapidly, did not make any fatal error in their conclusions about interest rate theory.

In sum, it appears that Keynes and his contemporaries had not gone far wrong in ignoring the issue of stocks versus flows. Both formulations of interest rate theory can handle the same phenomena and, assuming rapid adjustment of stocks, both formulations give equivalent results.

CONCLUSION

The liquidity preference versus loanable funds debate cast the liquidity preference theory in a poor light. At best it was seen to be nothing new, equivalent to the already existing loanable funds theory. At worst, it was seen to be seriously flawed. In the debate between Keynes and his contemporaries shortly after the *General Theory* was published, Keynes revealed confusion both about the loanable funds theory and about his own liquidity preference theory. That he did not have a completely thought-out and consistent theory became obvious as the loanable funds theorists raised questions to which he could give no satisfactory answers.

In the later debate, the liquidity preference theory suffered even more serious harm as it was reinterpreted into a form that turned out to be indefensible. By the end of the debate many of the contributors had come to agree on Klein's (1950a) dynamic interpretation. According to this interpretation of the theory, the interest rate is determined in a general equilibrium model that entails an adjustment process which says the interest rate changes whenever the excess demand for money is different from zero. The implication is that the interest rate can change even when there is an equilibrium in the bond market – an implication that does not make much economic sense.

The eagerness of the later economists to cast the liquidity preference theory within a general equilibrium framework led them to an interpretation that bears little resemblance to Keynes' original exposition of the theory. Keynes was explicit that his theory has the rate of interest determined by the supply of money relative to the demand for money in terms of bonds. Interestingly, he anticipated the confusion that might arise from the short-hand summary of the theory which says only that the interest rate is determined by the demand and supply of money.

> The liquidity-preference theory of the rate of interest which I have set forth in my *General Theory of Employment, Interest, and Money* makes the rate of interest to depend on the present supply of *money* and the demand schedule for a present claim on money in terms of a deferred claim. This can be put briefly by saying that the rate of interest depends on the demand and supply of money; though this may be misleading, because it obscures the answer to the question, demand for money in terms of what?
>
> (Keynes [1937] 1973, 14: 202)

Within Keynes' liquidity preference theory of interest,

therefore, if the interest rate is out of equilibrium, then so are both the bond and the money markets. But this is an implication which is at odds with both the static and the dynamic general equilibrium interpretations of the theory.

The liquidity preference versus loanable funds debate provides a good case study of the effect that mathematical modelling can have on economic discourse. The debate between Keynes and his contemporaries was conducted verbally and many confusions arose. It was hoped that by presenting the theories more rigorously, the issues might become clearer and yield to resolution. Our survey of the later debate, however, shows that the issues seemed to get more complex rather that clearer. The main problem appeared to be fixing on the appropriate mathematical analogues of the verbal theories. The participants differed, not so much on points of logic or fact, but rather on the mathematical specification of the theory. The debate serves well to demonstrate the difficulty associated with an attempt to translate a verbal theory into mathematics.

From the perspective of our restatement of the liquidity preference theory, much of the later debate is irrelevant. It proceeds within the context of a simultaneous equation general equilibrium model, rendering its results incommensurate with the results we obtain using an alternative approach. The earlier debate employs a mode of reasoning closer to our own. Our conclusion about the earlier debate is that, on most points, the loanable funds theorists were on stronger ground than Keynes. We share their choice of an analysis in terms of flows rather than stocks and we agree with their conclusion that it should make no difference whether one analyses the demand and supply of money or the demand and supply of loanable funds. The difference between our restated liquidity preference theory and the loanable funds theory as it is usually interpreted lies in our subsequent analysis of the loanable funds market. Our analysis leads to the conclusion that wealth-holders can dominate, so that their liquidity preferences, rather than the time preferences of savers or productivity considerations of producers, can be considered the determining factor of the interest rate.

Chapter 7

Intertemporal coordination and the liquidity preference theory of interest

The acceptance of a liquidity preference theory of interest forces one to reexamine the commonly held notion that the interest rate serves to allocate resources intertemporally through its coordination of saving and investment. This enduring idea informs much of the current discussion on topics such as the government deficit, the shortage of savings, and the low level of investment. To a large extent, however, the theory of inter-temporal coordination on which people base their policy judgments is only vaguely understood. Journalists, politicians and even some professional economists often appear as confirmation of Keynes' (1936: 383) remark about hard-headed practical people being slaves to some defunct economist. In this chapter, we wish to unearth the ideas of these defunct economists and examine them in the light of our liquidity preference theory of interest.

Our findings lead us to reject a powerful and ingeniously conceived aspect of the invisible hand of economic coordination. It is a part of the economist's understanding of the working of the capitalist system that was expressed intuitively by Adam Smith and which over the years has been refined and adapted in response to criticisms. Our general conclusion, however, is not completely nihilistic. We can still hold that intertemporal coordination will sometimes take place in individual markets through future prices if they exist, and through entrepreneurial expectations if they do not. What we argue against is only the notion of an interest rate mechanism coordinating the saving decisions of one set of individuals with the investing decisions of another.

DEFINING INTERTEMPORAL COORDINATION

One approach to gaining an understanding of the notion of intertemporal coordination is through an analogy with the less controversial notion of interspatial coordination. We might think of two towns not far from one another but remote from the rest of civilization. Suppose the demand for goods goes up in town A relative to the demand in town B. Town A experiences an unanticipated surge in population, say. Then we should find a shift of goods available for purchase from town B to town A. Prices will rise in town A and enterprising entrepreneurs will find a profit can be secured through shifting production so that more goods are available in town A and fewer are available in town B. A similar scenario is postulated in the idea of intertemporal coordination. One supposes that if demand for goods goes up in time A relative to time B, productive resources will shift so that there will be more goods coming on board in A than in B. The point at which the analogy breaks down, however, arrives when one specifies how the resources will be shifted. While in the theory of interspacial coordination we need only think of resources or goods being transported to another place, in the theory of intertemporal coordination the hypothesis is that the resources will be diverted towards more or less capitalistic methods of production. In the case in which demand shifts from the present to the future, the exact analogy would be simply to transport the resources through time – that is, to leave them unemployed. An outcome in which scarce resources are left un-exploited, however, is one of disequilibrium and is unacceptable to most economists. Similarly, in the case in which demand is shifted from the future to the present, the exact analogy would be for resources that would be exploited in the future to be exploited now. Again, the outcome is unacceptable. The reason this time is that the resources to be exploited in the future may not exist in the present. In order to better fit the circumstances, therefore, the theory of intertemporal coordination is extended to reach the postulate that investment spending will move in a direction opposite to consumer spending. This mechanism of inter-temporal coordination leads to a propitious balancing in the demands for productive resources. If fewer resources are required to produce for current consumption, then more resources are demanded to produce for future consumption.

A precise definition of intertemporal coordination is difficult because different economists have slightly different conceptions of it. We can, however, identify three related propositions, one at least of which enters into most discussions. The first is that a decision to change the rate of consumption out of current income – that is, to change the rate of saving – will lead to a decision to change the rate of investment in physical capital. The second is that a decision to change the rate of investment in physical capital will lead to a decision to change the rate of saving. And the third is that a decision to invest in physical capital requires, although may not lead to, a decision to save. For the sake of coherence, we shall focus primarily on the first proposition. The second is not as widely argued as the first and the third is not as controversial.

HISTORY OF THE IDEA

The idea of a causal connection between the decision to save and the decision to invest goes back at least as far as Adam Smith. He expressed it very simply:

> Whatever a person saves from his revenue he adds to his capital, and either employs it himself in maintaining an additional number of productive hands, or enables some other person to do so, by lending it to him for an interest, that is, for a share of the profits.
>
> (Smith [1776] 1937: 321)

Smith sums up his position in his famous quote that 'every prodigal appears to be a public enemy, and every frugal man a public benefactor' ([1776] 1937: 324). Smith's common sense notion of the mechanism persisted over generations of economists. There were critics (see Keynes 1936: 358–71) but they lay outside of the mainstream and, until Keynes, never commanded much of a following. Smith's followers strengthened his insights by explicitly specifying the rate of interest as the price that operates to coordinate the supply of saving with the demand for investment. The criticism that savings could be stashed under mattresses was accepted but the judgment was that this sort of behaviour was not widespread enough to affect the results much.

The real problem, however, with the Smithian notion of intertemporal coordination is not that people hoard their savings but rather that they put them in banks. Once a banking system is introduced the neat connection between the decision to save and the decision to invest is severed. Through their capacity to create credit, banks are able to finance new investment even when new saving is not forthcoming. Similarly, if business conditions are poor and prospective borrowers appear likely to default, banks can curtail the quantity of funds going toward new investment – again without any change in saving behaviour.

In his *History of Economic Analysis*, Schumpeter remarks that the idea of intertemporal coordination that Smith popularized (but which can be traced back to Turgot)

> proved almost unbelievably hardy ... the theory was not only swallowed by the large majority of economists: it was swallowed hook, line, and sinker. As if Law – and others – had never existed, one economist after another kept on repeating that only (voluntary) saving was capital creating.
>
> (Schumpeter 1954: 325)

The reason that economists held so firmly to the doctrine that Smith established may have been related to their reluctance to accept the idea of banks creating money. On this issue, Schumpeter (1954: 1113–17) claims that even as late as 1914 the money creating capacity of banks was not recognized in mainstream economic theory. (It may have been recognized as an institutional fact but it was a fact from which economic theorists chose to abstract.) In explaining the slow development Schumpeter writes:

> The reasons why progress should have been so slow are not far to seek. First, the doctrine was unpopular and, in the eyes of some, almost tinged with immorality – a fact that is not difficult to understand when we remember that among the ancestors of the doctrine is John Law. Second, the doctrine ran up against set habits of thought, fostered as these were by the legal construction of 'deposits': the distinction between money and credit seemed to be so obvious and at the same time, for a number of issues, so important that a theory which tended to obscure it was bound to be voted not only useless but wrong in point of fact – indeed guilty of the elementary error of confusing legal-tender money with the bookkeeping items that reflect contractual relations concerning this legal-tender money.
>
> (Schumpeter 1954: 1116–17)

It was during the Keynesian revolution that the idea that a decision to save will result in a decision to invest was under the most strain. Keynes revitalized the antagonistic notion of a paradox of thrift – the notion that through stepping up saving we diminish the total demand for goods and thus impoverish the economy. Keynes challenged the long-standing tradition with his ingenuous statement that

> an act of individual saving means – so to speak – a decision not to have dinner to-day. But it does *not* necessitate a decision to have dinner or to buy a pair of boots a week hence or a year hence or to consume any specified thing at any specified date. Thus it depresses the business of preparing to-day's dinner without stimulating the business of making ready for some future act of consumption.
>
> (Keynes 1936: 210)

From a writer with less authority than Keynes, this account might have been regarded as simple-minded – the sort of statement that would incite a failing grade in an economics examination. Keynes' reputation, however, carried the idea further and for a while it entered mainstream teaching.

Today Keynes has largely fallen out of fashion and less attention is given to the paradox of thrift. We find, even in the reputably Keynesian textbook by Samuelson and Nordhaus, the following account of the relation between saving and capital formation:

> But where do the resources needed to produce capital come from? Someone must be *saving* to provide funds for buying the capital goods. Someone must be abstaining from current consumption, thereby releasing resources needed to produce new capital goods. In a complex modern economy, with a sophisticated financial system like that of the United States, households and firms channel funds into capital goods by saving money in various financial assets. People buy bonds and stocks; they put money in saving accounts; they put money away for retirement in pension funds. All these are vehicles that carry funds from savers to the firms or people who buy capital goods.
>
> (Samuelson and Nordhaus 1989: 719)

Here we have a notion of intertemporal coordination that is

not far removed from the one expressed by Smith in the quotation above. The authors are simplifying, of course, and would, no doubt, provide the necessary qualifications if pressed for them. Still, it is significant that they have chosen this particular simplification and that in a detailed and relatively sophisticated undergraduate textbook, they have chosen to suppress any qualifications.

A belief in the kind of intertemporal coordination that Samuelson and Nordhaus describe underlies much of the journalistic discussion of economic policy issues. Repeatedly, one sees use made of the metaphor of a 'pool of savings' that can be drawn on by investors in physical capital. Investment is deemed to be low in the United States because the pool is relatively small and government deficits drain the pool of what saving there is. If only people would save more and the government would curtail borrowing, then the pool would swell, interest rates would fall, and investment in productive capacity would surge.

The view that more saving will not produce any tendency towards a higher level of investment in physical capital appears now to be a minority view. Among professional economists one sees it defended most often by the Post Keynesians. Unlike more mainstream Keynesians, this group views Keynes' contribution as posing a fundamental challenge to a macroeconomics rooted in the idea of the economy tending towards a general economic equilibrium. Davidson (1982) presents a Post Keynesian view of the matter in his discussion of what he calls the shortage of saving (SOS) hypothesis. He refers to an article in the financial press in which leading economic thinkers, including two Nobel prize winners and a former Chairman of the President's Council of Economic Advisors,[1] are quoted as saying that in order to increase productive capacity in the United States, the American people need to save more. The leading thinkers admit that, in the short-run, an increase in saving might be recessionary. But in the long run, they concur, investment will be higher.

For economists who work with neoclassical growth models, the idea that more saving means more investment comes naturally. For someone who doubts the relevance of the models, however, the result needs some other line of defence. Looking at it on the level of individual producers, it would seem that if consumers are cutting back on the demand for their output, they would be wise to scale back rather than increase their level of capital expenditure. Unless one is able to believe that the economy will get itself into a general equilibrium, the question of the process through which the decision to save leads the producer to decide to invest, needs to be addressed.

Davidson searches for an explanation but is unable to find one:

> the only logical sense that can be made out of the SOS hypothesis is that any policy which creates direct incentives for increasing private saving must simultaneously cause 'savers' to desire to hold their additional saving directly in the form of additional capital goods.
>
> (Davidson 1982: 47)

He does refer to the interest rate as a possible coordinator but dismisses it as a 'slender reed' (1982: 48) without expanding on why it would be ineffective. Yet if pressed for an explanation of the process, many economists would resort to a loanable funds theory in which the interest rate does the work. It is important, therefore, if one is to deny the importance of saving for investment, to confront the loanable funds theory.

THE LOANABLE FUNDS THEORY

There are two approaches that are commonly used to defend the position that a decision to save will lead to a decision to invest. There is the dualistic argument in which one says that in the short-run, interest is determined by the demand and supply of money, but that in the long-run interest is determined by the so-called real factors of productivity and time preference. One then says that it is through the real theory that we see how a decision to save results in a decision to invest. The dualistic approach appears to be the one adopted in the Samuelson and Nordhaus text. In one chapter the interest rate is shown to be determined by the demand for money relative to the supply (Samuelson and Nordhaus 1989: 347), but in another chapter a Fisher diagram (ibid.: 732–3) appears to explain the determination of the same variable. The dualistic approach is unsatisfactory, however, to someone committed to the causal process approach to economic analysis. It fails to indicate how the results of the short-run analysis translate into the results from the long-run theory. A complete causal process theory would begin with the short-run determination and show how forces work to create the tendencies towards the long-run position. Moreover, the dualistic approach fails to explain how it is that one can apply to the real world the implications about intertemporal co-ordination drawn from the equilibrium position of the long-run theory.

The other approach to defending the position that a decision to save will lead to a decision to invest is to integrate monetary factors with real factors in the form of a loanable funds theory. This theory was developed by a number of economists (see Robertson 1934, 1937, 1940; Ohlin 1937a, b; and Haberler [1939] 1958) at a time when it was thought incumbent to incorporate monetary factors into the theory of interest. Recognition of the money creating capacity of the banking system called into question theories in which capital was thought of as being saved and borrowed *in natura*. Briefly,[2] the loanable funds theory can be described as essentially a supply-of-saving-demand-for-investment theory of interest onto which monetary factors have been added. Thus, under one formulation, one can think of the demand for investment funds facing a supply of loanable funds which incorporates not only net saving[3] but also takes account of hoarding and changes in volume of bank credit. If one wanted to include the government sector then government borrowing could be added to the demand side and money creation to the supply side. The implication of the analysis is that the results of the supply-of-saving-demand-for-investment theory will apply as long as there is no change in hoarding, bank lending or government fiscal and monetary policy. If we have no reason to believe that changes in these factors are correlated with changes in the decision to save, then it seems fair to conclude that a change in the decision about how much to save will lead to an interest rate movement that will coordinate the change in the amount of saving with an equal sized change in amount of investment. The policy conclusion follows that increasing the rate of saving and reducing the deficit will, *ceteris paribus*, reduce the interest rate and increase the amount of investment.

The loanable funds theory, however, entails the limitation of static demand and supply analysis. Its results only apply to the equilibrium situation. Often, however, the questions that are posed require a dynamic theory. Take, for instance, the result that we have identified with intertemporal coordination that a decision to save will result in a decision to invest. While the loanable funds theory can only provide statements about relations between variables in equilibrium, this conclusion says something about economic agents acting through time. To arrive at it, one has to go beyond to confines of the static construction. Typically, an instructor in economics will do some hand-waving and tell a brief story about what economic agents are doing while he shifts the curves of a supply and demand diagram. In simple cases, he may not go too far wrong. But in the case of the highly complicated loanable funds market, it is important to be more systematic about the process through which the equilibrium is approached. In what follows, we shall take a causal process approach to analysing the question of the effect of a change in a decision to save and see if the results of a superficial dynamic interpretation of a loanable funds supply and demand diagram hold up.

Consider two identical economies A and B into which we introduce a change in the savings decision and then let us work out and compare the effect of the change on the two economies. Suppose Abigail in economy A decides to go from saving some of her income to saving it all, while her counterpart, Brigette, in economy B decides to go from saving some of her income to saving none. At the end of each payday Abigail goes to her bank to deposit her $500 wage, while Brigette heads to Macy's department store to spend hers. Abigail's bank then has $500 minus the required reserves to lend out. It would seem that Abigail's thrift has resulted in a greater supply of loanable funds in economy A. But consider what happens to the $500 that Brigette spends at Macy's. At the end of the day, Macy's will deposit the money into its bank, allowing that bank to lend out an additional $500 minus reserves. It is not clear that we have yet reached any difference in the supply of loanable funds in the two economies except for the short period of time that might elapse between when Abigail deposits the $500 and when Macy's does. One might argue that Abigail will be depositing her wage in a savings account with a relatively low reserve requirement and that Macy's will be employing a transactions account with a higher reserve requirement and thus through the differential in required reserves, there will be more loanable funds available in A. Today, however, the distinction between transactions and savings accounts has become increasingly blurred. In fact, a large banking customer like Macy's might have access to short-term instruments that would result in the $500 being lent out with no reserve requirements at all. It might, for example, have the money bundled up with its other deposits to be lent out on an overnight repurchase agreement.[4] Since on average the purveyors of consumption goods deal with more cash than do individual savers, it is not unreasonable to think that they are more likely to have access to the type of short-term instruments that allow banks to get around reserve requirements. Thus in the first round of effects it appears that Brigette's profligacy results in at least as many loanable funds being available as Abigail's thrift. Even in the longer term, as long as Abigail keeps her money in the bank, there are no grounds for supposing that her change in saving behaviour will have any clear effect on the loanable funds market. As far as the banks are concerned it makes little difference whether the money that swells the accounts of its customers are the result of someone's decision to save or someone's decision to spend.

If, with a loanable funds theory, we are to hope to get any difference in the two economies, we must assume that Abigail enters directly into the bond market, rather than assuming that she merely deposits her savings in a bank account. If she enters directly and exchanges her bank account for bonds, then it is clear that she is introducing a new supply of loanable funds. If the market was in equilibrium before she entered, then for the market to clear, the interest rate must fall to induce the marginal investor to borrow. A new equilibrium is reached when the interest rate has fallen and more money has been borrowed to finance new investment. Thus in economy A, Abigail's thrift has been shown to lead to the decision to invest more.

The problem with the above account of the matter is that it neglects an aspect of financial markets that we have argued, in a previous chapter, may be of decisive importance. It neglects the fact that a great deal of the activity in the bond market has nothing to do with new saving and new investment. The marginal bond seller may not be a firm trying to raise new funds but rather a wealth-holder who wants to sell bonds so that he can invest in something else. Similarly, the marginal buyer may not be someone who has done new saving but rather a wealth-holder who is cashing in another investment to buy the bond. The price of bonds is determined on the margin but this marginal trade does not appear in the loanable funds diagram.

Given the predominance of trading in existing assets relative to the flow of new issues, Abigail, in all likelihood, will buy her bond not from a firm expanding capacity but from a speculator who wants to sell the bond in order to invest in some other form of wealth. Whatever price they agree on will be determined not by productivity and thrift but rather by each party's uncertain expectation of future bond prices. Abigail does not want to pay a price which is high relative to what she thinks it might be in the future when she will want to sell; similarly, the seller will not want to sell at a price which he thinks is low relative to what he could get in the future. In order to buy a bond, Abigail needs to find someone whose expectation of the future price of bonds is less than her own.

The assumption of the loanable funds theory is that these speculative trades in existing issues can be ignored. Possibly they are thought to be a kind of noise causing random fluctuations in bond prices about a trend determined by the real factors. One must recognize, however, that the assumption is nothing more than an analogy with a phenomenon in wave theory. As such it may provide an avenue for research but cannot be considered a final argument.

If the increase in saving does not lead to an increase in investment in the short-run, that is, if we allow that in the short-run at least, speculative activity may obscure movement in what one believes is the underlying trend, then there may be a further problem for the theory. If investment does not come on board to replace the demand for consumer goods, then incomes will fall and the savings of those with the reduced incomes will fall as well. Thus Abigail's greater saving may be matched by less saving on the part of others, and her expansionary effect on the supply of loanable funds may be counteracted.

Still another problem with the loanable funds theory has to do with the difficulty of computing a demand for investment. If capital is a single substance, then there is no problem. The demand for capital can be treated like the demand for cold rolled steel coil, the quantity can be measured in terms of tonnes. Once we have different types of items, however, we are faced with the question of how to add them together. The loanable funds theory solves the problem by adding their money values together. But, as it has often been argued in capital theory debates, the prices of individual investment goods depend on the interest rate. At a low rate of interest, demand for investment goods will be brisk and prices will tend to go up. At a high rate, the prices will tend to fall. It would seem, then, that adding the prices of the individual capital goods together to get an aggregate demand for investment and using that concept to explain the rate of interest, involves some circularity. The loanable funds theory, which is supposed to explain the interest rate, has a demand curve that depends on the prices of capital goods which in turn depend on the interest rate. Demand and supply analysis proceeds by presenting a system of equations that can be solved so as to yield an equation for the unknown variables in terms of the known variables. In the case of the loanable funds theory, we have a situation in which one of the unknowns is the interest rate. In order to specify the demand equation, however, we must already know what that unknown is.

In sum, the loanable funds theory faces a number of problems. In addition to the conceptual problem of aggregating investment demands, problems arise when one takes a more detailed look at the processes through which an equilibrium is reestablished. We find that it is not clear from a loanable funds theory that a decision to save will lead to a decision to invest. First, there is the reasonable possibility that if savers deposit their money in a bank, then an expansion of the supply of loanable funds will not take place. Second, even if it is the case that savers enter directly into the bond market, it is not clear that the interest rate will be influenced immediately if speculative activity is going on at the same time, washing out the effect of the new saving. Moreover, if new investment does not come about shortly after the new saving, then incomes will fall, bringing aggregate saving with them. The result is that the decision to save more on the part of one person may be matched by the decision of another person to save less when his or her income has fallen.

HAYEK AND THE RICARDO EFFECT

While the loanable funds theory is arguably the most widely held theory used to justify the idea of intertemporal coordination, there is an alternative explanation developed by von Hayek (1939, [1942] 1948, [1969] 1978) which merits attention. An important part of the Austrian theory of the business cycle is what Hayek calls the Ricardo Effect – the theorem 'that in conditions of full employment an increase in the demand for consumer goods will produce a decrease of investment and vice versa' (Hayek [1969] 1978: 165-6). Hayek provides an original defence of the proposition but it was largely eclipsed by Keynes' work and today many economists are unfamiliar with it.

As a means of justifying an intertemporal coordination, Hayek's defence of the Ricardo Effect has some advantages over the loanable funds theory. First, it proceeds on microeconomic terms, avoiding some of the pitfalls of arguing in terms of aggregates. We mentioned in our discussion of the loanable funds theory above how the aggregate supply of savings is not associated in any simple way with individual decisions to save, since one's decision to save will affect other people's income and thus may cause them, in turn, to modify their plans to save. Hayek's theory avoids these difficulties because it does not resort to an aggregate supply of saving. In addition, by not resorting to an aggregate demand for investment, it avoids the problem of aggregating individual capital goods in a way that does not lead to circularity in the theory of the interest rate.

Another difficulty that we found with the loanable funds theory was that it ignored the fact that in the short-run, at least, the interest rate may be determined by speculative factors. The implication is that it cannot be relied on to send the appropriate signals and the process of intertemporal coordination will not be assured of getting off to the right start. We argue that if the process begins in the wrong direction, it is not clear that it will get back on track. Hayek avoids these difficulties by framing his theory so that it is the rate of profit, rather than the rate of interest, that does the coordinating. He maintains that in the long-run the rate of interest will fall into line with the rate of profit but realizes that on a day-to-day basis, the rate of interest is influenced by other forces (Hayek 1939: 67).

In his 1942 essay on the Ricardo Effect, Hayek introduces three concepts. First, he introduces the rate of turnover (T) which he defines as the number of times the money capital expended by a firm is received back again within the course of the year; second, the profit margin (M) defined as the proportional gain on each turnover of the money capital; and third, the internal rate of return (I) defined as the per annum percentage return on the money capital. Ignoring compound interest, the relationship between the three terms is

$I = TM$ or $M = I/T$

In equilibrium the internal rate of return will be equalized across firms. If, however, the price of output increases, then the internal rate of return of those firms with high rates of turnover will be higher relative to those firms with a low rate of turnover. Resources will be shifted to those firms, or to parts of a given firm, that have a high rate of turnover. Since, under Hayek's scheme, less 'capitalistic' processes of production have the lower rates of turnover, he achieves the result that an increase in the demand for consumption (or a fall in saving) leads to a decline in the provision of investment goods.

An example can be used to illustrate the theory. Consider two stores with different rates of turnover. On the one hand a small shop in the city centre close to its supplier, and on the other hand, a large suburban store. The small shop has little space so its manager replenishes the inventory ten times a year – suppose that ten times a year, he buys $10,000 worth of merchandise which he then sells with a 1 per cent margin before buying the next lot. According to Hayek's formula, his internal rate of return is 10 per cent. Space is plentiful but the cost of restocking is higher for the suburban store so it replenishes its inventory only twice a year. Suppose that twice a year it buys $50,000 worth of merchandise and sells it with a 5 per cent profit margin. As with the city shop, its internal rate of return is 10 per cent. Now suppose the demand for goods suddenly increases and prices of final output rise 5 per cent. The city store will have a profit margin of 6 per cent, raising its internal rate of return to 60 per cent, while the suburban store will have a profit margin of 10 per cent raising its internal rate of return to only 20 per cent. We see that the firm with less capital which turns it over a greater number of times a year gains more from the price rise than the more capitalistic firm with a lower rate of turnover. Hayek makes the point that we can think of a given firm with different parts of its capital associated with different rates of turnover. Thus one could think of rates of turnover that 'are 6 for the sums invested in current wages, 1 for the operating parts of the machines tools, etc., and 1/10 for the heavier machinery, buildings, etc.' ([1942] 1948: 229). Hayek's theory leads to the conclusion that in periods in which output prices have increased, firms' managers have an incentive to cut back on durable capital goods and invest more in working capital.

Hayek was at odds with the Keynesians in challenging their assumption that the yield of capital goods moves in the same direction as expected final demand. Keynes had emphasized entrepreneurial expectations of future profits as the determinant of their investment in physical capital. The implication is that when the demand for consumer goods is high, entrepreneurs are likely to be optimistic about future demand and will expand capacity; but when the demand is low, entrepreneurs will tend to scale back. Keynes' followers found Hayek's theory, which leads to the opposite conclusion, unconvincing. Joan Robinson gives an account of the reaction to Hayek's ideas about intertemporal coordination when he presented them as part of his theory of the business cycle at a seminar at Cambridge:

> R.F. Kahn, who was at that time involved in explaining that the multiplier guaranteed that saving equal investment, asked in a puzzled tone, 'Is it your view that if I went out tomorrow and bought a new overcoat, that would increase unemployment?' 'Yes', said Hayek 'But' pointing to his triangles on the board 'it would take a very long mathematical argument to explain why.'
>
> (Robinson 1980: 94)

If Hayek had to explain why without his triangles (which are not essential for the theory), he might have said, working under Kahn's assumptions of less than full employment and limited labour mobility, that buying the overcoat would induce entrepreneurs to work their existing sewing machines harder and employ more workers. Other factors of production would be shifted from making sewing machines to making coats. Workers in the sewing machine industry would be unemployed and there would be a reduction in demand by them for overcoats and other goods. The reduction in demand and the fact that there would be fewer sewing machines would lead to the unemployment. Hayek claimed that a transition from boom to bust would occur if there was not enough capital at the lower stages of production.

The point at issue between Hayek and the Keynesians was the importance of entrepreneurial expectations of future profitability relative to the importance of relative price changes. The

Keynesians thought Hayek was wrong to ignore the possibility that if demand is low, entrepreneurs may believe that they will not be able to sell what the extra capacity would produce. In Hayek's scheme entrepreneurs appear to behave mechanistically in response to relative price changes. From Hayek's perspective, however, the Keynesians appeared to focus on expectations and 'animal spirits' to the exclusion of all else. They did not seem to him to pay heed to the fundamental scarcity of capital. Their approach, if followed through consistently, would lead to a *reductio ad absurdum*.

> If it were true that an increase in the demand for consumer goods *always* leads to an increase in investment, even in a state of full employment, the consequence would be that the more urgently consumer goods are demanded the more their supply would fall off. More and more factors would be shifted to producing investment goods until, in the end, because the demand for consumer goods would have become so very urgent, no consumer goods at all would be produced.
>
> (Hayek [1969] 1978: 177)

Hayek is convincing on the point that investment could not be increased without limit but it is not so clear that it might not fall to zero without limit. If it were the case that consumer demand kept falling, it is conceivable that investment expenditures could continue to fall with it.

The Ricardo Effect is probably best thought of as two separate effects, each of which requires its own defence. On the one hand, there is what we might call the Ricardo Effect proper, that an increase in consumer demand leads to a fall in investment. On the other hand, there is what we could call the inverse Ricardo Effect, that a decrease in consumer demand leads to an increase in investment. The Austrian theory of the business cycle relies on the Ricardo Effect proper and does not require the inverse. Since the Ricardo Effect proper is more important, Hayek devoted most of his attention to it, leaving his position on the inverse unclear. He admits ([1942] 1948: 223n) in his most detailed statement of the theory that proving the Ricardo Effect proper does not prove the inverse, but he does not provide a separate proof of the inverse. And yet despite this admission, he continued to assert the inverse in his later writings (Hayek [1969] 1978: 165–6).

Quite apart from the Keynesian criticism of Hayek's defence of the Ricardo Effect, that it appears to ignore entrepreneurial expectations, there is the neoclassical criticism of the theory. Hayek's theory says that a change in the price of final output will lead to a change in the production process. A standard result from neoclassical price theory, however, says that if the prices of inputs relative to one another are unchanged then there should be no change in the optimal input mix. An increase in the price of output may cause firms to produce more but the optimal method of production will be the same. In response to the example we used to illustrate Hayek's theory, a neoclassical economist could argue that if the price of output is increased and the interest rate is unchanged, the large suburban store need not increase its rate of turnover and make more frequent trips to its suppliers in order to best benefit from the change. It needs only to borrow more, expand the store, and increase the size of each turnover.

Hayek agreed with the theory behind the neoclassical objection ([1942] 1948: 221) but did not believe that it constituted a fatal criticism. His main response was that as a practical matter, firms do not face a completely elastic supply curve for credit. As they become more indebted they are perceived as less credit-worthy and the risk premium attaching to the interest rate charged them increases. This credit rationing assumption, however, is open to criticism. Blaug (1985: 545) cites 'the familiar fact that as much as 50–75 per cent of corporate investment relies on internal sources in the form of retained profits and unused depreciation accruals'. The implication is that the equity in a firm increases when it is expanding. Thus, even if it is borrowing more, it may not be perceived as any riskier since its debt–equity ratio will not necessarily have increased.

Hayek does provide reasons ([1942] 1948: 250–1), however, why the Ricardo Effect would exert its influence even if the supply of credit were perfectly elastic at a constant rate of interest. One point that he raises is that entrepreneurs are uncertain about whether the high output prices will continue into the future. To continue our example, by the time the suburban store has enlarged its facility to accommodate a larger inventory, the super-normal profits might have been bid away already. Hayek (ibid.) cites 'the principle of "making hay while the sun shines"' as a reason for adopting the less capitalistic method. He notes that since producers realize that they are in a state of disequilibrium, they are uncertain as to

which of the various elements in the picture will change so as
to create a new equilibrium situation . . . . [Thus] the more
elaborate preparations for future profits at a lower rate
(though higher in aggregate) and involving greater risk will
not appear as attractive.

(Hayek [1942] 1948: 250–1)

In the above line of defence of the Ricardo Effect, Hayek
appears to be providing a good illustration of the cogency of two
methodological tenets that are usually associated with the Post
Keynesians. First he recognizes that decisions formed in an
environment of uncertainty will be different from those that
would be made if the future was known, and second, that production takes time so that it is unreasonable to suppose the
equilibrium configuration of prices and quantities will be reached
quickly. If entrepreneurs expected higher output prices to
continue, they would behave as the neoclassicals suppose and
expand capacity replicating existing plant and equipment. But
because they are uncertain about the future and because
installing new capacity takes time, they are more likely to work
existing equipment harder, delay maintenance and installation of
new capital and bring old equipment back into use than they are
to make long-term plans to expand. The conclusion is that when
the demand for consumer goods rises, one cannot be assured that
the demand for investment goods will follow. It may even be the
case that investment that was planned before demand suddenly
increased will be deferred until demand has slowed. The policy
implication is that in the short-run, expansionary fiscal policy
which stimulates consumption will not necessarily be beneficial
for investment and may even be detrimental. In the long-run,
however, if entrepreneurs have become convinced that the higher
level of demand will persist, they have an incentive to expand.

Unfortunately, Hayek cannot employ the same type of
argument for the inverse Ricardo Effect. When the demand for
final output falls, he maintains that the price of output falls and
producers invest more in physical capital. Since Hayek did not
give as much attention to this direction of the Ricardo Effect, it is
not clear how he would defend it. He could argue that in times of
low consumer demand, firms will compete more vigorously for
market share and in an effort to lower costs or improve quality
they might deepen their capital structure. But again the

neoclassical question arises: why, if a change in the input mix could improve profitability, did the producers not institute it before? Hayek's position could be justified only if we assume the producers were tending towards a more capitalistic equilibrium before the change in output price and that the change accelerated their movement towards it, increasing their rate of investment.

Yet even with this justification, two other problems remain with the inverse Ricardo Effect. Hayek's insistence that we pay attention to the risk premium on loans appears to work against him in the case of reduced output prices. If a firm is showing poor profits, then lenders will be more reluctant to lend and the firm will be forced to pay a higher rate of interest if it is to expand its operation. The credit rationing thesis that Hayek proposed as an answer to why firms would not expand when output prices are high can also be employed to discredit his contention that firms will expand when output prices are low.

Working against him, as well, is Hayek's admission that the day-to-day interest rate appearing in the financial markets may be different from the rate of profit. If the interest rate happens to be above the rate of profit when demand falls off, not only will firms not borrow for expansion, they may even take retained earnings that were destined to replace existing capacity and invest them in financial instruments. If the poor business climate had left them hesitant about going forward with plans for new plant and equipment, this strategy would allow them to defer their decision until they were more confident about the future business prospect.

There appears an asymmetry in the theory of the Ricardo Effect. Arguing that investment will decline when demand for consumer goods increases is easier than arguing that investment will increase when the demand for consumer goods declines. In the case of an economy close to full employment, it is clear that if the demand for consumer goods increases something has to give. Even the Keynesians would admit that stimulating consumption in a fully employed economy would not be conducive to investment. Hayek, however, provides an insight that is not commonly referred to in debates about saving and investment. Hayek's insight is that even if the economy is not fully employed, rising consumption may lead firms to increase their output as quickly as possible through working existing equipment harder. The result of their efforts will be a shallowing of the capital structure. The implication is that, even in cases of less than full employment, economic policy aimed at stimulating consumption may be detrimental to capital formation in the short-run. In this respect, Hayek's analysis leads to the same conclusion as the loanable funds theory while avoiding the attendant conceptual problems with that theory.

CONCLUSION

If one is to accept a liquidity preference theory of interest of the sort that we present in previous chapters, then one is forced to abandon the idea of the interest rate serving to coordinate the demand for consumer goods relative to the demand for producer goods. The idea that we have labelled intertemporal coordination says that there are forces in the economy that cause the demand for producer goods to move in a direction opposite to the demand for consumer goods.

In this chapter, we examine closely the loanable funds theory – probably the most widely held theory of the mechanism. We find that if one attempts to give the theory a causal process interpretation, several problems arise. From the perspective of our liquidity preference theory, Hayek's defence of the Ricardo Effect appears a more promising route towards developing a theory of intertemporal coordination. Close scrutiny of his theory, however, finds it lacking, as well. We are led to the seemingly nihilistic position of denying any mechanism that assures an intertemporal coordination. We can still allow that in markets for individual goods, coordination through time might be facilitated through future prices if they exist, or through entrepreneurial expectations if they do not. An example of the latter is an entrepreneur who looks at demographic data in order to predict the future demand for his product and plans his capital investments accordingly. The notion we reject is only that in general a decision to save will be translated into a decision to invest.

A general intertemporal coordinating mechanism serves economic theory well by easing the reestablishment of a general economic equilibrium when it is disrupted by a change in the desire to save. When a change in saving decisions is effected, the mechanism directs resources from one sector of the economy to the other. If the decision is to save more, resources move from consumer goods industries to the producer goods industries; *vice versa* if the decision is to save less. Without the coordinating mechanism the reestablishment of a general equilibrium is more complicated and less likely to occur.

Consider an economy with four scarce goods: labour, nets, fish and some non-reproducible good that serves as unit of account and medium of exchange. Suppose people decide to cut back on consumption and their demand for fish falls. As the fish market gets into equilibrium, fishermen are laid off. Now the labour market is out of equilibrium. As the price of labour falls, the fish industry substitutes fishermen for nets to produce the lower quantity of fish. Now the net market is out of equilibrium and net makers are laid off. And so the process continues. In each market we assume flexible prices and a tendency towards equilibrium but we find there is no mechanism that ensures all the markets are in equilibrium at the same time. A general equilibrium model might be able to tell us the configuration of prices that would constitute an equilibrium but it gives us no idea of the process that gets the economy there.

Without the intertemporal coordinating mechanism the disequilibrium in the consumer goods industry arising from a change in saving decisions can spread to the producer's goods industry with the result that the economy moves further away from, rather than closer to, a general equilibrium. It is true that with the passing of enough time and without any further exogenous changes, all the individual markets might happen to clear simultaneously. It is not obvious, however, what the new general equilibrium will look like. We cannot say with much assurance that the increased propensity to save will lead to a situation with fewer consumer goods and more producer goods. One cannot rule out the possibility that prices will have adjusted so that even if people are saving a greater proportion of their incomes, the same combination of capital and labour produces the output.

To reject the idea that the interest rate serves to coordinate intertemporally does not imply a totally nihilistic approach to economic theory that says that since everything is in a constant state of flux there is no hope for any deductive economic reasoning. One can still accept that in individual markets – in the markets for welders, overcoats, hairdressers, loanable funds, etc. – there are equilibrating tendencies. One can even accept that sometimes in some markets something approximating an equilibrium exists. But one must be a little more sceptical about the possibility of a general equilibrium in which all scarce resources are fully employed.

Many models employed by economists to study the problems of capital accumulation and economic growth, however, assume that the economy is in a continuous state of general equilibrium. The models show clearly that a high level of saving is associated with a high level of investment and the policy prescription that usually follows is that to increase productive capacity it is necessary to motivate people to cut back on their consumption. Our analysis sheds doubt on that line of reasoning. We are left in the minority camp of the Post Keynesians who seem to be alone in both professional and popular opinion in denying that the supposed problem of a low level of capital accumulation has to do with a shortage of saving.

The minority opinion stands against what seems to many as common sense. If we want more resources to be directed towards the production of investment goods, then it is necessary to direct them away from the production of consumer goods. We must recognize, however, that this is a necessary, not a sufficient, condition. It does battle with another necessary condition, that the entrepreneurs who decide on the investment expect that it will be profitable. A state of slack consumer demand would tend to work against the belief that new investment could be profitable. Even if the entrepreneur himself were confident, his creditors might not be and the risk premium added to the interest rate charged might make the investment prohibitive.

The dominance of models that assume that the economy reaches a general equilibrium provides part of the explanation for why the notion of the interest rate serving to coordinate intertemporally has persisted. Another reason is that the results of the theory appear to be confirmed by experience. When consumer demand is high it is true that interest rates often rise and investment spending is curtailed. Exactly what the loanable funds theory would predict. For every empirical regularity, however, there is usually more than one theory that can explain it. The phenomenon of high interest rates associated with low saving could be explained by arguing that the increase in consumer demand causes economy to reach close to maximum output. The result is that inflationary pressures build and an inflationary premium is worked into the interest rate. If the inflationary premium was perceived as a statistical expectation of future inflation, then firms might go ahead and borrow anyway knowing that it is a fair bet they could cover the interest costs through the higher price of their product.

But the inflationary premium arguably overstates the inflation that occurs:[5] it will do so if it incorporates some compensation for increased uncertainty associated with lending in terms of the unit of account in an inflationary environment. Moreover, firms behave like speculators in deferring borrowing until interest rates are at what they believe to be a low level. A time in which interest rates have increased with an inflationary premium may not be perceived as the best time. Similarly, in a recessionary environment in which borrowing is low, interest rates may be low because of a reduction in the inflationary premium. The rejection of the idea of the interest rate producing an inter-temporal coordination calls for a new look at the macroeconomic issues of capital accumulation and growth. We shall not venture here to propose a solution to these problems. Post Keynesians (see Davidson 1982: 55) who share our scepticism about the mechanism are inclined to advocate a policy of encouraging consumption and easing finance to produce maximum growth. This policy stance, however, is not a necessary implication of a rejection of the belief that the interest rate serves to coordinate intertemporally. It relies on the additional assumption that all the necessary factors of production are standing ready to be employed. If there are shortages of, say, skilled workers, the policy of stimulating demand and easing finance may lead to bottlenecks and increased prices.

Chapter 8

Concluding summary

> I am more attached to the comparatively simple fundamental ideas which underlie my theory than to the particular forms in which I have embodied them, and I have no desire that the latter should be crystallised at the present stage of the debate. If the simple basic ideas can become familiar and acceptable, time and experience and the collaboration of a number of minds will discover the best way of expressing them.
>
> (Keynes [1937] 1973, 14: 111)

The liquidity preference theory of interest first came to light in Keynes' *General Theory*. There Keynes coined the term liquidity preference and presented the novel thesis that this preference plays an important role in the determination of the interest rate. As we indicate in Chapter 5, however, Keynes' presentation of the theory is problematic. While many economists have decided that its flaws justify it being rejected altogether, other economists continue to be intrigued by it. The highly elusive Chapter 17 of the *General Theory* in which Keynes presents his theory in terms of own-rates of interest, especially continues to stimulate research (see Kregel 1980; Chick 1983; Nell 1983).

Like these authors, we believe there is something valuable in Keynes' theory of the interest rate. But rather than simply trying to patch up what we take to be the flaws in his theory, we start afresh. From Keynes we take a few 'comparatively simple fundamental ideas' and develop them in a new way. Our approach is arguably more radical than that normally taken by Keynesian interpreters and one might conclude that what we have done is not close enough to what Keynes intended to be called an interpretation of his theory. To claim complete originality, however, would be to claim far too much. We might best characterize the present work as a reinterpretation whose standard is not so much consistency with Keynes' writings but persuasiveness in its own right. Our goal is to present a theory of interest that is logically consistent and empirically plausible. Further work in subjecting aspects of the theory to empirical tests is necessary but the first task is to see how all the pieces fit together – to bring the whole picture into focus. Without the theoretical groundwork, the results of empirical tests can be misleading.

The standard method for economic theorists in the post-war period has been the simultaneous equation general equilibrium model. In taking Keynes' prose presentation of his liquidity preference theory and fitting it into a general equilibrium model, mathematical economists believed that they were imbuing it with more rigour. Our view is that much was lost in the mathematical transformation of the theory. The mathematical method does not aim at providing a coherent explanation that allows one to 'make sense' of the phenomenon under question. Rather the aim is to generate falsifiable predictions that can be tested against carefully measured empirical facts. The extent to which the predictions are verified provides the means of evaluating the theory. What is lost through this methodology, however, is the kind of causal explanation that is found in other social sciences. Our position is that the contribution the liquidity preference theory makes to our economic understanding cannot be expressed in the kind of models that dominate today in economics. We adopt, therefore, the alternative, much older tradition in economic theory of presenting the analysis in verbal causal terms.

One can view the present work as taking up the debate in interest rate theory that was ground to a standstill by the introduction of the mathematical method. Earlier in this century, economists debated fervently about the root cause of interest. One group held that the productivity of capital was the ultimate explanation, another group that the explanation lay in the impatience to consume, and still another group that it was a combination of the two factors acting together. In Chapter 3, we develop arguments against the idea that the productivity of capital and impatience are the root causes of interest. Most of our arguments against the two determinants are not original and can be found in the earlier debate. Our innovation is in the constructive part of the chapter in which we argue that liquidity preference is a factor that was overlooked in the earlier controversy. It appears that both the impatience and productivity proponents were right in what they denied but wrong in what they affirmed.

The reason the factor of liquidity preference escaped notice was most likely due to the standard practice of abstracting from money in developing theories of exchange value. Money was seen as a mere intermediary in exchange. Neoclassical price theory taught that the fundamental factors generating exchange value were preferences and scarcity and it was believed that focussing on the monetary basis of transactions could obscure these fundamental factors. We agree that for many aspects of the theory of price, abstracting from money can be useful and not dangerously misleading. In the theory of interest, however, it may have led economists to neglect a potentially fruitful line of analysis. Besides acting as a medium of exchange, money serves the purpose of transferring purchasing power through time. As a store of value, money has an important advantage over other assets. Its liquidity allows one the assurance that its full value can be readily obtained so that if an unexpected contingency or opportunity arises, one is better able to react to it. If market participants derive a psychic yield from liquidity, then there will be a premium on present dollars over future dollars, that is, a rate of interest.

The insight that liquidity preference provides an explanation for the existence of interest is central to the theory of interest that we are presenting, but it is not the complete theory. Our main task is accomplished in Chapter 4 in which we set out a simplified cash–debt market and show how the various factors operating in that market interact. The aspect of our simplified cash–debt market that leads us to our distinctive results is the attention we pay to speculative trading.

Traditionally, speculation is abstracted from in the theory of interest. The rationale is that speculative activity is responsible only for short-run fluctuations in the interest rate and that the more important question is what explains the level around which the fluctuations take place. Coddington (1983: 81) provides the image of a pot of boiling soup. The speculation can be likened to the heat causing the surface to bubble but one has to appeal to the quantity of soup and the dimensions of the pot to understand the level above which the bubbling is occurring. Our response to the Coddington objection is that insofar as speculation is a component of liquidity preference, it does play a role in explaining not just the bubbling but the level, as well. We argue that one of the reasons behind a liquidity preference is a general speculative motive. This motive springs from the idea that some opportunity – although one is not sure exactly what – might emerge and that if such an opportunity does emerge, one is in a better position to seize it if resources are held in liquid form. Given the close ties between the notion of speculation and liquidity preference, abstracting from speculation in a liquidity preference theory would be to defeat the purpose. Speculation is viewed as integral to the theory of interest and not something whose influence can be factored in afterwards. Moreover, if one begins one's theory of interest by assuming away speculative behaviour, then one will be led to the conventional conclusion that interest is determined by the interaction of saving and investment – but only by default. If one removes speculative traders from the cash–debt market, then all one is left to work with is saving and investment.

Besides the general speculative motive that leads one to desire liquidity because some unexpected opportunity might arise, we identify what we term the particular speculative motive, which operates when one believes one can profit from 'knowing better than the market' (Keynes 1936: 170) the future course of some investment. Thus, for example, if one believes that the interest rate will rise in the future, one will maintain a liquid portfolio and wait for the rise to occur. Unlike the general speculative motive, the particular speculative motive does not necessarily generate a desire for liquidity. If one believes that the interest rate is at a peak, then one will want to invest in debt. Often, however, the general and the particular speculative motive will be operating in concert. Even the most confident investors will harbour some doubts about the accuracy of their predictions. Thus, even if investors believe strongly that interest rates have reached a peak, they may maintain some liquidity just in case an unexpected future rise does occur.

The particular speculative motive is not unique to the cash–debt market. In understanding the determination of the price of many assets that serve as stores of value, the particular speculative motive needs to be considered. Investors will often pay exorbitant prices for assets because they believe their values will rise even further. In a real estate boom, for example, property values may climb above what the expected future stream of rents justifies. Buyers are willing to suffer a low rate of return from holding property because they are expecting a compensating capital gain when they sell. Eventually, however, a turning point will be reached and some investors will find their expectations disappointed. When the speculative fever fades away, property values will more likely reflect their ultimate usefulness as homes, factories, shops, and so on. Then, with the benefit of hindsight, one can conclude that a speculative bubble had occurred.

With a piece of property or a company stock, one can compute a price–earnings ratio and get some notion of whether there is a speculative component, or bubble, in the price. In other markets, however, discerning when a speculative bubble exists is more difficult. Some assets, for instance, generate yields that are psychic and thus impossible to measure. Consider, for example, paintings by Vincent van Gogh which sell for millions of dollars. The buyers of such paintings no doubt appreciate their aesthetic value. It is possible, though, that they are willing to pay such high prices only because they expect they would be able to recoup their investment if they had to sell. In formulating their offer, therefore, they may be consulting not just their utility function but also their uncertain expectation of what the painting would sell for in the future. It is impossible to compute, however, how much of the price is attributable to the psychic yield that its owner derives and how much is attributable to the speculation of what it would sell for in the future. Since it is difficult to discern when a speculative premium, or bubble, is present, any bubble that does exist is less likely to burst. The pressure for a bubble to burst usually comes from those investors who see that prices are out of line with the fundamentals that are the ultimate source of an asset's value, but in the case of assets whose yields are psychic, the fundamentals can elude analysis.

Our liquidity preference theory claims that the cash–debt market is closer to the market for van Gogh's paintings than it is to the real estate market. The liquidity that cash provides has a psychic yield that is difficult to measure, just as with a van Gogh. Moreover, just as with a van Gogh, the interest rate may contain, at any point in time, in addition to the amount reflecting its psychic value, a component due to the particular speculative motive. Unlike in the real estate or stock market, there is no tendency for this component to be eroded. Therefore, one cannot justify abstracting from speculation. Just as explaining the price of a van Gogh canvas by appealing only to its aesthetic value would be to miss a possibly important part of the explanation, a theory of interest cannot proceed by ignoring the particular speculative motive.

Sufficient has been said in defence of the position that a realistic theory of interest ought to recognize the role of speculation, both general and particular, in the bond market. The more controversial step in the liquidity preference theory is in drawing out all the implications of the speculative decisions. Our method in Chapter 4 is to introduce changes in the desire to save on the part of consumers, in the investment opportunities facing producers, and finally in the liquidity preferences of wealth-holders. We then work out the effect that these changes will have on the interest rate. We attempt to show that the introduction of speculative trading can put a spanner in the works of the mechanism that is supposed to coordinate saving and investment. If speculative trading is operating, then when there is an increase in the desire to save, say, producing a contractionary pressure on the level of aggregate income, the interest rate may not fall sufficiently to cause a countervailing rise in investment. Without a mechanism whereby decisions to save are matched by decisions to invest, the level of total income can vary. The implication is that a balance between saving and investment can be achieved without any further change in the interest rate. In the case of an increased desire to save, total income can fall, implying that the level of aggregate saving need not rise. Thus, an increased level of investment is not necessary for saving and investment to be in balance. Moreover, the idea that the interest rate adapts to changes in the marginal efficiency of capital needs to be reexamined. We show that it is plausible that when the marginal efficiency of capital is out of equilibrium with the interest rate, the equilibrating process leads to changes in stocks and prices of capital goods which ultimately lead to an adjustment in the marginal efficiency of capital, rather than in the interest rate (Rogers 1989: chap. 9).

With regard to the theory of interest, economists have for a long time been under the influence of a powerful analogy. The interest rate is thought of as the price that coordinates the supply of saving with the demand for investment, just as the price of shoes coordinates the supply of shoes with the demand for shoes. The analogy is extended to incorporate speculative trading. If speculators foresee a change in one of the fundamental factors behind the price of shoes – in the availability of leather, for instance – they will attempt to buy up existing stocks and drive up their price. Speculation, then, is seen as an activity that causes the new equilibrium to be reached more quickly. If speculators turn out to be wrong about the shortage of shoe leather, the price will fall and speculators will suffer a loss. Speculators are viewed as servants to the real factors, rather than agents in their own right. In setting out our liquidity preference theory, one of our major tasks is to show on theoretical grounds why this commonly accepted analogy is inappropriate for the bond market.

In giving up the idea that the interest rate serves as a lever producing an increase in the demand for investment goods when there is a fall in the demand for consumer goods and *vice versa*, one must reexamine the idea of the economic system as a whole tending towards a general equilibrium in which individual markets equilibrate simultaneously. If consumers want fewer goods in the present, we are without the usual mechanism whereby the unemployed factors and raw materials will be absorbed into the investment goods industry. Equilibrating tendencies in one market can exacerbate a disequilibrium in another. Admittedly, the problem does not arise in a one-commodity world, nor in a world of continuous market clearing. When these extreme assumptions are made, a different theory of interest and intertemporal coordination might apply. A more realistic analysis, however, might be better if it gave up on the idea of a general equilibrium and worked instead only with the idea of equilibrating tendencies in individual markets.

The most important macroeconomic implication of our liquidity preference theory is the doubt that it casts on the notion that policies designed to increase the willingness to save, or to reduce the budget deficit, will lead, through a reduction in the interest rate, to more investment in physical capital. First, our contention that the profitability of capital is a consequence and not a cause of interest leads us to reject the idea that a lower interest rate necessarily means more investment, over the long-run. It is true that producers do act as speculators and wait until the interest rate is low relative to what is considered a normal level to issue debt. A temporary fall in the interest rate can, therefore, stimulate borrowing, causing producers to concentrate their borrowing in the period in which the interest rate is low. If the interest rate is permanently lowered, however, market pressures will cause the change to be reflected in the prices of capital goods, meaning the investment is no more profitable than before. An analogous situation is one in which a town decides to stimulate its housing market by lowering property taxes. Houses already on the market, whose asking prices did not reflect the new property tax rate, might sell more briskly. Competitive pressures, however, would cause housing prices to rise to reflect the lower property taxes. In sum, we question whether, even if an increased desire to save led to lower interest rates, the result would be more investment spending over the long-run.

The more fundamental criticism of the notion that the level of productive investment can be increased by encouraging saving is our position that the interest rate will not necessarily fall in response to increased thriftiness. It is true that insofar as an increased desire to save has a contractionary effect on the total level of economic activity, any inflationary premium that is factored into the interest rate might be reduced. The part of the interest rate beyond the inflationary premium, on the other hand, will not necessarily fall. Our analysis suggests that other factors may dominate in its determination. We do not go as far as arguing that saving ought to be discouraged. One cannot deny that in a closed economy operating near capacity, if resources are being diverted to provide for present consumption, then there are fewer resources left for investment. A certain level of saving can be regarded, therefore, as a necessary condition for a high level of investment. Our analysis suggests only that it is less than a sufficient condition.

Notes

1 INTRODUCTION

1 Early on Shackle attempted to formalize his insights about uncertainty and apply them to the liquidity preference theory (Shackle 1961b: 241–51). But later he was to admit (Shackle 1983: 6) that such attempts were misguided.
2 See pp. 70–1 for further discussion of the assumption that the interest rate is a policy variable.

2 METHODOLOGY AND DEFINITIONS

1 Some economists, however, interpret Marshall's method differently (see Rogers 1989: 184–6).
2 We are using the term speculative motive in a sense more general than that in which Keynes used it. Keynes (1936: 171) uses it to refer only to bear speculation in the bond market.
3 The definition involves an approximation. The exact relationship is that the nominal interest rate is equal to the real rate plus the rate of inflation plus the product of the real rate and the rate of inflation.

3 THE THEORY OF INTEREST FROM AN 'ESSENTIALIST' PERSEPCTIVE

1 Essentialism as a philosophical doctrine has several interpretations which should not be confused with the interpretation, employed by a few economists, that we are following here.
2 Our analysis is not sensitive to the definition of capital that one chooses to employ. The same arguments would apply if the word 'capital' was replaced by 'waiting' or 'time'.
3 We ought to note that the logical difficulties involved in ascribing a causal role to the physical or value productivity of capital invalidate the argument that it is a combination of impatience and capital productivity that gives rise to interest.

4   A CAUSAL PROCESS ANALYSIS OF EQUILIBRIUM IN THE CASH–DEBT MARKET

1   We shall use the term wealth-holder to refer to the person who manages the wealth, whether it be the owner or someone working on the owner's behalf, for example, a mutual fund manager.
2   Some (see Malkiel 1981: 20) prefer to use the term speculation to refer only to trading done with the intent of making short-term gains. The problem with this approach is specifying accurately the length of the short term.
3   'The typical dealer is running a highly levered operation in which securities held in position total 500 to 600 times capital' (Stigum 1983: 281).

5   KEYNES AND THE LIQUIDITY PREFERENCE THEORY OF INTEREST

1   We are assuming a closed economy with no government expenditure or taxation. The result follows from the familiar accounting identity $Y = C + I = C + S$, where Y is national income, C is aggregate consumption, I is aggregate investment, and S is aggregate saving.
2   See Chapter 3 for a more complete discussion of the problems with productivity explanations.
3   The letter was amongst the papers discovered in a laundry basket in 1976 when Lady Keynes vacated Tilton. It has been suggested that these papers are important because they 'almost certainly represent documents that Keynes had set aside to have with him while he was re-writing' (Keynes 1979).
4   It was amongst the papers in the famous Tilton laundry basket.

6   THE LIQUIDITY PREFERENCE VERSUS LOANABLE FUNDS DEBATE

1   Robertson's version of the theory is immune from Lerner's criticism for another reason. He defined saving as the excess of last period's income over this period's consumption, and thus severed the necessary equality of saving and investment.
2   It ought to be noted that Keynes was using the terms *ex ante* and *ex post* in a different sense from the other participants in the debate. Ohlin, for example, used the terms to refer to desired and actual quantities respectively.
3   Hahn (1955) reaches a similar conclusion about the difference between the liquidity preference and loanable funds theories.
4   Hicks (1986: 125) himself was later to admit that his early analysis of the debate was 'superficial'.

7 INTERTEMPORAL COORDINATION AND THE LIQUIDITY PREFERENCE THEORY OF INTEREST

1   Franco Modigliani, Robert Solow and Martin Feldstein.
2   For a more detailed discussion of the literature see the chapter above on the loanable funds versus liquidity preference debate.
3   Net saving is equal to new saving minus dissaving and minus borrowing for consumption.
4   In a repurchase agreement Macy's bank would use Macy's money to buy a Treasury security and then agree to sell it back the next day, at a slightly higher price. In effect, the money is being lent out overnight.
5   That inflationary premia usually overstate the inflation which ensues explains why real, as well as nominal, interest rates will rise when consumer demand is high.

References

Ackley, G. (1957) 'Liquidity preference and loanable funds theories of interest: comment', *American Economic Review*, 47, 5: 662–73.

Addleson, M. (1986) '"Radical subjectivism," and Austrian economics', in I.M. Kirzner (ed.) *Subjectivism, Intelligibility and Economic Understanding*, New York: New York University Press.

Arrow, K.J. and Hahn, F.H. (1971) *General Competitive Analysis*, San Francisco: Holden Day.

Blaug, M. (1985) *Economic Theory in Retrospect*, 4th edn, Cambridge, England: Cambridge University Press.

von Böhm-Bawerk, E. ([1914] 1959) *History and Critique of Interest Theories*, vol. I of *Capital and Interest*, trans. G.D. Hunke and H.F. Senholz, South Holland, Ill.: Libertarian Press.

—— ([1912] 1959) *Positive Theory of Capital* and *Further Essays on Capital and Interest*, vols II and III of *Capital and Interest*, trans. G.D. Hunke and H.F. Senholz, South Holland, Ill.: Libertarian Press.

Brown, H.G. (1913) 'Marginal productivity versus the impatience theory of interest', *Quarterly Journal of Economics*, 27, 630–50.

—— (1914) 'The discount versus the cost of production theory of capital valuation', *American Economic Review*, 4, 340–9.

Brunner, K. (1950) 'Stock flow analysis: discussion', *Econometrica*, 18, 247–51.

Chick, V. (1983) *Macroeconomics After Keynes: A Reconsideration of the General Theory*, Oxford: Philip Allan.

Coddington, A. (1983) *Keynesian Economics: The Search for First Principles*, London: Allen & Unwin.

Cuthbertson, K. (1985) *The Supply and Demand for Money*, Oxford: Basil Blackwell.

Davidson, P. (1965) 'Keynes' finance motive', *Oxford Economic Papers*, 17, 47–65.

—— (1978) *Money and the Real World*, 2nd edn, London: Macmillan.

—— (1982) *International Money and the Real World*, New York: Halsted Press.

Dolan, E.G. (ed.) (1976) *The Foundation of Modern Austrian Economics*, Mission, Kansas: Sheed & Ward.

Duffie, D. and Sonnenschein, H. (1989) 'Arrow and general equilibrium theory', *Journal of Economic Literature*, 27, 565–98.

Fellner, W. and Somers, H.M. (1941) 'Alternative monetary approaches to interest theory', *Review of Economics and Statistics*, 23, 43–8.

—— (1949) 'Note on "stocks" and "flows" in monetary interest theory', *Review of Economics and Statistics*, 31, 145–6.

—— (1950a) 'Stock flow analysis: comment', *Econometrica*, 18, 242–5.

—— (1950b) 'Stock and flow analysis: note on the discussion', *Econometrica*, 18, 252.

Fetter, F. ([1902] 1977) 'The "roundabout process" in the interest theory', in M. Rothbard (ed.) *Capital, Interest and Rent: Essays in the Theory of Distribution*, Kansas City: Sheed, Andrews & McMeel.

—— (1904) *Principles of Economics*, New York: Century Company.

—— ([1914] 1977) 'Interest theories, old and new', in M. Rothbard (ed.) *Capital, Interest and Rent: Essays in the Theory of Distribution*, Kansas City: Sheed, Andrews & McMeel.

Fisher, I. (1907) *The Rate of Interest*, New York: Macmillan.

—— (1930) *The Theory of Interest*, New York: Macmillan.

Friedman, M. (1953) 'The methodology of positive economics', in *Essays in Positive Economics*, Chicago: University of Chicago Press.

Haberler, G. ([1939] 1958) *Prosperity and Depression*, revised edn, Cambridge, Mass.: Harvard University Press.

Hahn, F.H. (1955) 'The rate of interest and general equilibrium analysis', *Economic Journal*, 65, 52–66.

—— (1973) 'The winter of our discontent', *Economica*, 40, 322–30.

Hansen, A. (1953) *A Guide to Keynes*, New York: McGraw Hill.

Hausman, D.M. (1981) *Capital, Profits and Prices: An Essay in the Philosophy of Economics*, New York: Columbia University Press.

Hawtrey, R.G. (1937a) 'Rejoinder to "alternative theories of the rate of interest"', *Economic Journal*, 47, 436–43.

—— (1937b) *Capital and Employment*, New York: Longmans, Green & Co.

von Hayek, F.A. (1939) *Profits, Interest and Investment*, London: George Routledge & Sons.

—— ([1942] 1948) 'The Ricardo effect', *Economica*, 11, N.S. 34: 127–52, reprinted in *Individualism and Economic Order*, Chicago: University of Chicago Press.

—— ([1969] 1978), 'Three elucidations of the Ricardo effect', *Journal of Political Economy*, 77, 2, reprinted in *New Studies in Philosophy, Politics, Economics and the History of Ideas*, Chicago: University of Chicago Press.

Hicks, J.R. (1936) 'Mr Keynes' theory of employment', *Economic Journal*, 66, 238–53.

—— (1937) 'Mr Keynes and the classics; a suggested interpretation', *Econometrica*, 5, 147–59.

—— (1939) *Value and Capital*, Oxford: Oxford University Press.

—— (1967) *Critical Essays in Monetary Theory*, Oxford: Clarendon Press.

—— (1974) *The Crisis in Keynesian Economics*, New York: Basic Books.

—— ([1976] 1983) 'Time in economics', in A.M. Tang, F.M. Westfield and J.S. Worley (eds) *Evolution, Welfare and Time in Economics*, reprinted in

John Hicks, *Money, Interest and Wages: Collected Essays on Economic Theory*, vol. II, Cambridge, Mass.: Harvard University Press.

—— (1977) *Economic Perspectives*, Oxford: Clarendon Press.

—— (1979) *Causality in Economics*, New York: Basic Books.

—— (1980–1) 'IS–LM: an explanation', *Journal of Post-Keynesian Economics*, Winter 1980–1.

—— (1986) 'Loanable funds and liquidity preference', *Greek Economic Review*, 8, 125–31.

Holton, G. (1973) *Thematic Origins of Scientific Thought*, Cambridge, Mass.: Harvard University Press.

Jaffé, W. (ed.) (1935) 'Unpublished papers and letters of Leon Walras', *Journal of Political Economy*, 187–207.

—— (1983) *Essays on Walras*, ed. D. Walker, New York: Cambridge University Press.

Johnson, H.G. (1951–2) 'Some Cambridge controversies in monetary theory', *Review of Economic Studies*, 19, 93–104.

—— (1961) 'The General Theory after twenty-five years', *American Economic Review*, Papers and Proceedings of the 73rd Annual Meetings, 51, 2: 1–17.

Kahn, R.F. (1954) 'Some notes on liquidity preference', *The Manchester School of Economic and Social Studies*, 22, 3: 229–57.

Kaldor, N. (1960) 'Keynes' theory of the own-rates of interest', in *Essays on Economic Stability and Growth*, Glencoe, Ill.: Free Press.

Kauder, E. (1957) 'Intellectual and political roots of the older Austrian school', *Zeitschrift fur Nationalokonomie*, 17, 411–25.

Kaufman, H. (1986) *Interest Rates, the Markets, and the New Financial World*, New York: Times Books.

Keynes, J.M. (1936) *The General Theory of Employment, Interest and Money*, London: Macmillan.

—— (1930) *A Treatise on Money*, London: Macmillan.

—— (1973) *The Collected Writings of John Maynard Keynes*, ed. D. Moggridge, vols 13 and 14, London: Macmillan.

—— (1979) *The Collected Writings of John Maynard Keynes*, ed. D. Moggridge, vol. 29, London: Macmillan.

Kirzner, I. (1990) 'The pure time-preference theory of interest: an attempt at clarification', in L.H. Rockwell, Jr. (ed.) *The Meaning of Ludwig von Mises*, Auburn, Ala.: Ludwig von Mises Institute.

Klein, L.R. (1950a) 'Stock flow analysis in economics', *Econometrica*, 18, 236–41.

—— (1950b) 'Stock flow analysis: further comment', *Econometrica*, 18, 246.

—— ([1947] 1966) *The Keynesian Revolution*, London: Macmillan.

Knight, F.H. (1941) 'The business cycle, interest, and money: a methodological approach', *The Review of Economics and Statistics*, 23, 2:53–67.

Kregel, J.A. (1980) 'Expectations and rationality within a capitalist framework', paper given at the Annual Meeting of the American Economic Association, Denver, Colorado.

—— (1982) 'Money, expectations and relative prices in Keynes' monetary equilibrium', *Economie Appliquée*, 35, 3: 449–65.

—— (1983) 'Effective demand: origins and development of the notion', in J. Kregel (ed.) *Distribution, Effective Demand and International Relations*, London: Macmillan.

Kuhn, T.S. (1970) *The Structure of Scientific Revolutions*, 2nd edn, Chicago: University of Chicago Press.

Lachmann, L. (1937) 'Uncertainty and liquidity preference', *Economica*, 4, 295–308.

—— ([1950] 1977) 'Economics as a social science', in W.E. Grinder (ed.) *Capital, Expectations, and the Market Process*, Kansas City: Sheed, Andrews & McMeel.

Lavington, F. (1921) *The English Capital Market*, London: Methuen.

Lavoie, M. (1984) 'The endogenous flow of credit and the Post Keynesian theory of money', *Journal of Economic Issues*, 18, 771–97.

Leijonhufvud, A. (1968) *On Keynesian Economics and the Economics of Keynes*, New York: Oxford University Press.

—— (1981) *Information and Coordination*, New York: Oxford University Press.

Lerner, A.P. (1936) 'Mr Keynes' "General Theory of Employment, Interest, and Money"', *International Labour Review*, 33, 4: 435–54.

—— (1938) 'Alternative formulations of the theory of interest', *Economic Journal*, 48, 211–30.

—— (1944) 'Interest rate theory – supply and demand for loans or supply and demand for cash', *Review of Economics and Statistics*, 26, 88–91.

—— (1952) 'The essential properties of interest and money', *Quarterly Journal of Economics*, 66, 2: 172–93.

McGregor, P.G. (1985) 'Professor Shackle and the liquidity preference theory of interest rates', *Journal of Economic Studies*, 12, 89–106.

Malkiel, B.G. (1981) *A Random Walk Down Wall Street*, 2nd college edn, New York: W.W. Norton.

Mayer, H. (1932) *Der Erkenntniswert der funktionellen Preistheorien* in *Wirtschaftstheorie der Gegenwart*, vol. II, Vienna: Springer.

Menger, C. ([1883] 1963) *Problems of Economics and Sociology*, trans. F. Nock, ed. L. Schneider, Urbana, Ill.: University of Illinois Press.

Mill, J.S. ([1848] 1909) *Principles of Political Economy*, ed. W.J. Ashley, London: Longmans, Green, & Co.

von Mises, L. (1949) *Human Action: A Treatise on Economics*, New Haven: Yale University Press.

Modigliani, F. (1944) 'Liquidity preference and the theory of interest and money', *Econometrica*, 12, 1: 45–88.

—— (1963) 'The monetary mechanism and its interaction with real phenomena', *Review of Economics and Statistics*, 45, 79–107.

Moore, B.J. (1988) *Horizontalists and Verticalists: The Macroeconomics of Credit Money*, New York: Cambridge University Press.

Mott, T. (1985–6) 'Towards a post-Keynesian formulation of liquidity preference', *Journal of Post Keynesian Economics*, 8, 2: 222–32.

Nell, E. (1983) 'Keynes after Sraffa: the essential properties of Keynes's theory of interest and money', in J. Kregel (ed.) *Distribution, Effective Demand and International Relations*, London: Macmillan.

O'Driscoll, G. and Rizzo, M.J. (1986) 'Subjectivism, uncertainty, and rules', in I. Kirzner (ed.) *Subjectivism, Intelligibility and Economic Understanding*, New York: New York University Press.

Ohlin, B. (1937a) 'Some notes on the Stockholm theory of savings and investment I', *Economic Journal*, 47, 53–9.

—— (1937b) 'Some notes on the Stockholm theory of savings and investment II', *Economic Journal*, 47, 221–40.

—— (1937c) 'Rejoinder to "alternative theories of the interest rate"', *Economic Journal*, 47, 423–7.

Pasinetti, L. (1974) *Growth and Income Distribution: Essays in Economic Theory*, New York: Cambridge University Press.

Patinkin, D. (1948) 'Relative prices, Say's Law, and the demand for money', *Econometrica*, 16, 135–54.

—— (1949) 'The indeterminacy of absolute prices in classical economic theory', *Econometrica*, 17, 1–27.

—— (1958) 'Liquidity preference and loanable funds: stock and flow analysis', *Economica*, NS 25, 300–18.

—— (1976) *Keynes' Monetary Thought: A Study of its Development*, Durham, North Carolina: Duke University Press.

Pellengahr, I. (1986) 'Austrians versus Austrians I: a subjectivist view of interest' and 'Austrians versus Austrians II: functionalist versus essentialist theories of interest', in M. Faber (ed.) *Studies in Austrian Capital Theory, Investment and Time*, New York: Springer-Verlag.

Robertson, D.H. (1934) 'Industrial fluctuation and the natural rate of interest', *Economic Journal*,44, 650–6.

—— (1936) 'Some notes on Mr Keynes' general theory of employment', *Quarterly Journal of Economics*, 51, 168–91.

—— (1937) 'Rejoinder to "alternative theories of the rate of interest"', *Economic Journal*, 47, 428–36.

—— (1938) 'Mr Keynes and "Finance"', *Economic Journal*, 48, 314–18.

—— (1940) *Essays in Monetary Theory*, London: P.S. King and Son.

Robinson, J. (1961) 'Own rates of interest', *Economic Journal*, 71, 569–600.

—— (1980) *Collected Economic Papers*, vol. 4, Cambridge, Mass.: The MIT Press.

Rogers, C. (1989) *Money, Interest and Capital: A Study in the Foundations of Monetary Theory*, New York: Cambridge University Press.

Samuelson, P.A. (1967) 'Irving Fisher and the theory of capital', in W. Fellner (ed.) *Ten Studies in the Tradition of Irving Fisher*, New York: John Wiley and Sons.

—— (1981) 'Schumpeter as an economic theorist', in H. Frisch (ed.) *Schumpeterian Economics*, New York: Praeger Publishers.

—— and Nordhaus, W.D. (1989), *Economics*, 13th edn, New York: McGraw–Hill Books.

Sargent, T. (1979) *Macroeconomic Theory*, New York: Academic Press.

Schumpeter, J.A. ([1911] 1961), *Theory of Economic Development, An Inquiry into Profits, Capitalism, Credit, Interest and the Business Cycle*, trans. R. Opie, New York: Oxford University Press.

—— (1954) *History of Economic Analysis*, ed. Elizabeth Boody Schumpeter, New York: Oxford University Press.

Scitovsky, T. (1940) 'A study of interest and capital', *Economica*, N.S. 7, 293–317.

Seager, H.R. (1912) 'The impatience theory of interest', *American Economic Review*, 2, 834–51.

Shackle, G.L.S. (1949) 'The nature of interest rates', *Oxford Economic Papers*, NS 1, 100–20.

—— (1961a) 'Recent theories concerning the nature and the role of the rate of interest', *Economic Journal*, 71, 209–54.

—— (1961b) *Decision, Order and Time in Human Affairs*, Cambridge: Cambridge University Press.

—— (1967) *The Years of High Theory: Invention and Tradition in Economic Thought 1926–1939*, New York: Cambridge University Press.

—— (1972) *Epistemics and Economics*, Cambridge: Cambridge University Press.

—— (1974) *Keynesian Kaleidics*, Edinburgh, Scotland: Edinburgh University Press.

—— (1983) 'An interview with G.L.S. Shackle', *Austrian Economics Newsletter*, 4, 1.

Smith, A. ([1776] 1937) *The Wealth of Nations*, ed. Edwin Cannan, New York: Random House.

Stiglitz, J. (1977) 'Discussion of the paper by Professor Malinvaud and Mr Younes', in G.C. Harcourt (ed.) *Microfoundations of Macroeconomics*, Boulder, Colo.: Westview Press.

Stigum, M. (1983) *The Money Market*, 2nd edn, Homewood, Ill.: Dow Jones: Irwin.

Tobin, J. (1958) 'Liquidity preference as behavior towards risk', *Review of Economic Studies*, 25, 65–86.

Townshend, H. (1937) 'Liquidity-premium and the theory of value', *Economic Journal*, 47, 157–69.

Tsiang, S.C. (1956) 'Liquidity preference and loanable funds theories, multiplier and velocity analysis: a synthesis', *American Economic Review*, 46, 4: 539–64.

—— (1957) '"Reply" to Ackley', *American Economic Review*, 47, 673–8.

—— (1966) 'Walras' Law, Say's Law and liquidity preference in general equilibrium analysis', *International Economic Review*, 7, 3: 329–45.

—— (1980) 'Keynes's "finance" demand for liquidity, Robertson's loanable funds theory and Friedman's monetarism', *Quarterly Journal of Economics*, 94, 467–91.

Weintraub, E.R. (1982) *Mathematics for Economists: An Integrated Approach*, New York: Cambridge University Press.

Wray, L.R. (1990) *Money and Credit In Capitalist Economies: the Endogenous Money Approach*, Brookfield, Vt: Edward Elgar.

Yeager, L.B. (1979) 'Capital and the concept of waiting' in M.J. Rizzo (ed.) *Time, Uncertainty and Disequilibrium*, New York: Lexington Books.

Young, W. (1987) *Interpreting Mr Keynes: the IS–LM Enigma*, Cambridge, England: Polity Press.

Index